MW00880221

A Trace Element

By

John Ritter

© 2002 by John Ritter. All rights reserved.

No part of this book may be reproduced, stored in a
retrieval system, or transmitted by any means,
electronic, mechanical, photocopying, recording, or
otherwise, without written permission from the author.

ISBN: 1-4033-1686-4 (e-book)
ISBN: 1-4033-1687-2 (Paperback)

Library of Congress Control Number: 2002091206

This book is printed on acid free paper.

Printed in the United States of America
Bloomington, IN

Cover Design: Whisper

1stBooks - rev. 07/12/02

Acknowledgements

My grateful appreciation to my friends and family, this book's earliest readers. You believed in me and encouraged me. Thank you to Denise Meadows and Dickie Moriella, Cathy Hunt Briscoe, Linda Brown, Mollie McCarthy, Lou Holmin, Jennifer Vrana, Susie Goodall, Sandy and Jerry Ave, Jim Barber and Diane Butler, Michelle Bertepelle, Sheila and Ron Donald, Joan and Nelson Stewart, Donna Holmin, Robin Kelly, Timothy Davis, Katie Fennema, Vincent and Virginia Ritter. Thank you to my colleagues who supported me at work. And especially, thanks to Roger Holmin, you are the wind beneath my wings. Without you, there would be no book.

1

Miami

Monday, June 21, 1999

THE LANDING GEAR of the Boeing 757 snaps into place as the jet noses toward the runway at Miami International Airport. The plane vibrates as it touches the asphalt, then stops at the gate a few minutes later. The captain turns off the fasten seatbelt sign. American Airlines Flight 68 from Dallas-Fort Worth has been routine. As part of the flight crew, I will have a three-hour break and then fly home to Washington, DC.

Passengers pull their baby strollers and overstuffed bags from overhead bins. They edge toward the exit. "Bah bye," I say from my station just behind the first-class cabin. The crew call bell rings. I pick up the inter phone.

"John, a flight service manager is here to meet you," says Michelle Bertapelle, the lead flight attendant.

How odd, I think.

I squeeze my way up the aisle. Debbie, from the Miami flight service office, hands me a piece of American Airlines stationery, localized with a swaying palm tree on the top. My name is written on it, along with the name and phone number of a doctor and a flight service manager from my home base.

I look at it puzzled. *There must be a family emergency back home.*

"You need to call the doctor," she says.

Debbie leads me to the phone at a nearby gate. Agents are busy checking in passengers headed to vacations in the Caribbean. I'm not that swift with telephones. I fumble as I dial the call.

"Dr. Yiannou? This is John Ritter. I was asked to call you."

"I'm sorry to inform you that you have had a positive drug test, for cocaine," he says. "You're being removed from your trip."

"That can't be," I finally stammer. "I have never done drugs. There is a terrible mistake."

"You should call your union, if you are member," the doctor says. "Also, you can contact Cindy Buff at Corporate Medical if you have questions." I find a pen in my pocket and write down the phone number.

"Are you taking any prescribed medication?" the doctor asks.

My mind is exploding. I can remember only two of the three medications I take daily. I am suffering from some big time shock. My hands are shaking. I feel the blood draining from my face.

Debbie, from flight service, stands there two feet away. She sees I'm in a severe state of confusion.

"We can go to my office if you would like to make phone calls," she offers.

"Sure. I need to call the union and I want to call home."

We head to the jet bridge to retrieve my luggage from the airplane. The other flight attendants walk out the door, pulling my Roller board suitcase.

"Are you okay?" Michelle asks. "Is everything all right?"

"There's been a terrible mistake but I'll be okay," I reply, as Debbie leads me away.

Debbie's office turns out to be a cubicle. It is only slightly more private than the ticket counter where I got the *big news*. I hear people talking and laughing on the other side of the thin partition. *Everyone must know I'm in trouble for a drug test.* First, I dial the union phone number.

I hear Juan's voice, but it's just a recording. "Hello. This is Juan Johnson, chair of the Washington, DC, base. Sorry I can't take your call right now but please leave your name and a message."

I leave a pretty desperate sounding message.

I call the headquarters number for the Association of Professional Flight Attendants (APFA) in Dallas and leave a second message for Juan. I call Cathy Petraglia, our vice chair. Again no answer so I leave another message. To hear myself telling people I tested positive for cocaine is beyond my wildest imagination. I feel like I'm in someone else's body. I don't deserve this. I don't understand this. I feel tears building up behind my eyeballs. I refuse to cry.

Next I call the other name on the "note" from flight service, the manager-on-duty back at Washington National Airport. I tell her my dilemma and ask if she'll be meeting me on arrival home. Later, I learned this was a fairly significant breach of my own confidentiality. Flight Service supposedly is never notified of a positive drug test by medical, only that a removal from service has occurred.

"I'll be gone home by the time you get here," she tells me.

Finally, I call home and reach a real person. Roger, my partner of 10 years, is cool and levelheaded when under fire, feisty when he's been messed with and highly motivated when he's challenged. He knows my telephone call is highly irregular. He is floored by my news.

"I will continue to try to reach Juan and Cathy," he offers. Roger, also a flight attendant, is a union representative at a competing airline. He handles dozens of calls from flight attendants with problems. His job is to right the errors and sift through procedures and policy to make sure flight attendants are treated fairly. "I can meet your flight when you get to Washington." he offers.

"That's not necessary," I reply. "I can make it home okay." But I knew, in my heart, that he would be there for me. I sit back and take a deep breath. *I need to think calmly.*

Debbie sticks her head in the cubicle to check on me.

"I'm done with the phone. How am I getting home?"

"You're listed on the next flight to Washington National. It leaves in about 45 minutes. Are you ready to go to the gate?" she says. "Do you want me to walk down with you?"

"No. That won't be necessary. I can find my own way. But thanks."

If I ever needed my Marlboro Light 100s, this was the moment. I head outside to curbside to collect myself. I take a long drag. *What do I know about cocaine? Not much. How could this possibly happen to someone like me, pretty much a lightweight, never drink more than two or three beers, never liked marijuana when I tried it in college 25 years ago.*

Knowing I would be subject to random drug testing was the easiest part of entering an airline career. I didn't have to give up anything.

I hadn't thought twice about my random test last week. When my number is up, I pee in the cup and head for home. I have been drug tested three or four times before and it was no big deal–a minor inconvenience at the end of a trip for which flight attendants receive $10 in pay. I tossed my copies of the paperwork on the bedroom dresser that night and forgot about it. I may have mentioned in passing to Roger that I had a drug test.

It is time to march! In a fog, I drag myself to the gate and check in for my last flight home. *Do all these people know what is wrong here?* I turn around to see two crewmembers I've been traveling with for the past two days, Pete Wolbart and Michelle Bertapelle. Until we arrived in Miami, it was a relaxing and enjoyable trip.

Pete is a cool guy, proud father of two. All month I've enjoyed hearing stories of his two boys. His three-year-old Kevin had dialed up 911 one morning. Pete's wife was surprised when the police showed up at the door. Pete had showed me pictures and plans for the backyard playhouse he would build this summer.

Both Pete and Michelle are easy to work with. They are competent at the job and I've known them both for five or six years. I feel comfortable with them. I'd trust my life in their hands in the event of an emergency. I don't know them outside work but it's been an enjoyable two days. Michelle and Pete had checked on board the airplane, looking for me. They were worried about my mysterious and sudden departure.

"I'm being sent home. My random drug test from last week came back positive for cocaine."

We stand there in a state of disbelief. Across the gate area, the ticket agent at the jet bridge door waves impatiently. It is departure time and he is ready to close the door.

I hurry on board, walk all the way to row 26 and slide across two empty seats to the window. White-faced, I can't hide the grim, sinking feeling in my gut. I feel like I've been punched in the stomach. I don't feel much like "Something Special in the Air."

Since Michelle and Pete already had been on board, the working crew knows something is amiss. I'm wearing the same crisp white shirt, blue uniform and gold wings, pulling the familiar crew luggage. We've never met before, but there is an immediate sense of concern for a distressed coworker. They finish their safety demonstration and stop at my row. When they ask, I tell. I have nothing to hide.

BY THE TIME I arrive home, both Cathy Petraglia and Juan Johnson, from my union, have returned my calls and talked to Roger. I call Cathy, who tells me she will get the forms to me tomorrow that I need to order the split sample tested. I call Juan, who's out of town, on her cell phone.

"I can't believe it," Juan says. "I've known you for a long time. There is something wrong here. I believe you, that there is a mistake. Call me anytime you need to talk to someone."

By now it's midnight. Roger and I are mentally drained. We've set an agenda of phone calls we'll make in the morning, starting with my personal physician.

We head to bed. Sleep eludes me. I lie there awake. In a few short hours my life has taken a terrible, dramatic turn. My good reputation could be tarnished and airline career is at stake. Just last month, my horses were the center of my life.

2

Dorothy, you're not in Kansas anymore.
-- The Wizard of Oz

JUST THREE WEEKS EARLIER on Memorial Day Weekend, Roger and I had finished our second rodeo of the year. The clouds churned in the sky over the Oklahoma State Fairgrounds. The sun peeked over the horizon. Thunder rumbled in the distance. It was 6 am and the temperature was dropping. Still drowsy, we stuck our heads out of the living quarters of our horse trailer.

The hot, humid air was still. The sky looked haunting. Are those funnel clouds in the distance? Roger turned on the radio to find a weather report. Where do we seek shelter? A nearby ravine is probably full of rats. Time to roll out of Tornado Alley. Fresh in our minds was the twister destruction we saw four days earlier, a strip mall leveled, sheet metal hung up in trees, houses missing roofs.

I brewed a pot of coffee and rolled up the awning on the trailer. We packed up our traveling gear and prepared the horses for the two-day trip home to Virginia. We liked to sleep in the morning before leaving but this day we felt a sense of urgency.

In five years, our rodeo competition riding has greatly improved. Both of us posted our best times ever in Oklahoma and the year ahead looked promising.

The horses were our passion and traveling with them was our adventure. All three had distinctive personalities and looks. Sizzler, my Sorrel gelding, was tall and athletic, with one white sock. A blaze running down his face swept over one nostril, giving the allusion that his nose was crooked. Sizzler was a pussycat until you put a saddle on him to run. Even then, he was quiet until he saw the arena and heard other horses running. Then he shifted into competition mode, anxious and ready to race.

Little Man Go, Roger's flashy tricolor paint horse we call Paint, was smaller, sought attention and liked to be the boss in the field at home. He was a willing worker that copped a little attitude on days when he was pushed. Paint had finally recovered from a serious injury when he fell on a barrel run six months ago. He's not the fastest horse around but he's always the prettiest.

Honey, the newest member of our "family," is a short, dark Bay mare with coal black legs and a small white spot on her forehead. She is fast and we've not yet pushed her near her potential. She's been in Arkansas for the past month to be bred to a powerful, high-speed barrel-racing stallion. We were excited about having a baby in 11 months. I've just learned to rope off her. I'm lucky to not rope my own cowboy hat but I'm determined to improve my skills.

On this day, we had an extra passenger, Jennifer Vrana, a cowgirl and friend from Philadelphia. She flew into Oklahoma City but was riding back to the East Coast with us. It's not unusual in the rodeo world to be giving a lift to another competitor, or their horse for that matter.

Jennifer boarded her horse, Quinn, with ours back in Maryland and we saw her frequently. She was under the weather with an ear infection. She was sleeping a lot, even when she was riding shotgun to the driver. The person in that seat is supposed to keep the driver awake, read the map and manage navigation. We called her Sleeping Beauty.

Hours later, we pulled our rig through middle Tennessee, soon to pull off I-40 for an overnight at a boarding stable outside Lebanon. It was our third trip through Tennessee this year and we talked about pulling up our stakes on the East Coast and moving here. The rocky hills were beautiful as we passed farms with silos, white painted fences and livestock grazing peacefully. The location was central to many of our travels with the horses. Friends in the area were trying to sell us on Nashville as a great city.

"Picture this," Roger imitated, doing his best version of Sophia from television's *Golden Girls.* "Sicily...A log home with our horses out back. I was thinking we should put our house on the market and move. I'm calling the realtor when we get home."

"It's worth thinking about," I replied.

The next evening we arrived at the farm near Upper Marlboro, MD, where the horses have their own 15-acre field and a small three-stall barn. They were glad to be home after being on the road for a week, bucking and racing across their field, rolling in the dirt. We noticed that Honey has a bit of mucous in her eye. We should have our veterinarian check her if it doesn't go away soon.

Within days, real estate agent Mary Wharton was sitting at our kitchen table. She was our agent two years ago when we bought the house and she was excited about getting our business again. Roger surprised me with her visit, though it wasn't unexpected. We discussed a sale price and listing prices of other homes in the neighborhood. The market was good, but not hot. We have time, we figure. We signed to list the house.

A Century 21 New Millennium® For Sale sign was stuck in the flowerbed out front. Our four-level colonial-style townhouse was located within a stone's throw of George Washington's Mount Vernon. Mary had prepared listing sheets, piled on the coffee table in the center of the living room for prospective buyers.

We had lived in the house just two years. If we got our asking price, we'd get everything out that we put into it. We never built a deck off the kitchen and never landscaped the backyard. The property was comfortable but it was still just a house, not a home. We liked it but we were ready to move on.

Our jobs as flight attendants allowed us to live somewhere other than our base cities. We each had 10 years seniority at our respective carriers and that gave us more scheduling flexibility. We would both have to commute from Nashville. Likely, I would be based in New York; Roger would commute to Philadelphia. That would be a small sacrifice to reduce our cost of living and to have our horses in our back yard rather than around the dreadful Capitol Beltway in another state. Moving to the country had been a dream for a year or two.

A WEEK LATER, Linda Taylor, our veterinarian, checked our mare for a second time. Now Honey had a temperature of 102.6, an egg-size lump growing under her chin, and a foul odor to her mouth. Dr. Taylor suspected strangles, a highly contagious disease that can be fatal. She ordered a regiment of penicillin and sulfa tablets, a form of antibiotic.

Five days later, Dr. Taylor told us it is almost certainly strangles, a disease that infected the lymph glands and was often characterized by a cloudy, yellow puss draining from the nostrils. In bad cases, the extreme swelling would cause the horse to strangle to death.

Honey had a "flutter" when she breathed and Dr. Taylor suspected that she had an abscess in her throat. She increased the penicillin dosage to 35 cc twice a day, ordered strict stall rest for the patient and drew a syringe of blood for confirmation cultures.

"What about the baby?" I wondered.

"It's hard to tell at this point," Dr. Taylor said. "She is very sick and she had a high temperature which could cause her to absorb the fetus. Getting her better right now is our first priority."

Dr. Taylor also ordered our horses quarantined to their own field, no riding with other horses on the farm and no contact with other horses for the next month. The ugly disease will spread through direct contact with other horses or can be carried on the hands or clothing of humans caring for the horses. Extreme caution is the rule of the day. No local barrel racing competitions this summer. We are disappointed. Plans to haul the horses to a rodeo in Omaha late in June are out the window.

That evening, I smashed up a prescribed number of chalky-white sulfa tabs and placed the powder in baggies. This made for convenient feeding when we're gone on trips and not caring for the horses ourselves.

"These look like little bags of cocaine," Roger joked when he saw them on the kitchen counter at the farm.

THREE DAYS LATER, I was in a van with two other flight attendants, riding to the layover hotel in downtown Dallas. At the hotel, I checked in, asked for a smoking room and headed for some needed rest. I checked my messages at home and listened to Roger.

"Your horse is sick. I'm on my way to our field to give him penicillin. I'm on the cell phone. Call me," he said frantically.

That evening, we talked four times. Sizzler was running a fever of 102 and refused to eat, uncommon in a healthy horse. Roger gave a lackadaisical Sizzler bute, an aspirin-like medicine that helps reduce fever, and he talked to the vet who would check him tomorrow.

I felt helpless. I flipped the channels on the TV remote control. Nothing caught my interest. I tried to read a book but my mind was at home.

"Now I have two sick horses," I worried out loud to Pete, my fellow flight attendant, on the crew van to the airport early the next morning. It's a dilemma, the sick child syndrome, and any parent worries about it when work takes you away from home overnight.

Dr. Taylor checked Sizzler and Honey, taking Honey off the sulfa tabs since the culture showed lack of sensitivity to it. She ordered penicillin for Sizzler along with Honey. Honey continued to gradually improve. She was bright and alert now. We're supposed to check their temperatures twice a day and call Dr. Taylor if they go over 102.

That evening I arrived at Washington National Airport. The crew call bell rang. My number for random drug testing was up. I followed a supervisor to the medical station, peed in the cup and signed the many pages of paperwork. Random drug testing became federal law for airline workers in 1988 with the Department of Transportation providing guidelines and each company setting specific policies. About a fourth of the work force is tested every year for marijuana, cocaine, opiates, phencyclidine (PCP) and amphetamines. Employees are selected randomly.

I casually watched the collector, Thomas Hyde, as he completed the required forms. I initialed seals that go on the two containers of urine that will be shipped to a testing lab. I headed to the crew parking lot and pushed the drug test to the back of my mind as I looked forward to my day off.

3

"Failure isn't falling down. It's staying down."
–R Holmin, needlepoint hanging on our kitchen wall

Alexandria, VA.
Tuesday, June 22, 1999

I SMELL fresh-brewing coffee downstairs. It lures me from sleep. Did I just have a bad dream? The clock radio shows it's 7 am. Last night really happened. I was told I had a positive drug test for cocaine.

Roger is already awake, working the phone, a skill he has honed as a union rep, seeking answers, interpreting contracts, getting to the people who make decisions and changes. He has even hooked an electronic taping device to the telephone so he can record important conversations to transcribe later. As a child, Roger would carry a notebook in his pocket and keep records of his siblings' activities. They nicknamed him The Detective.

Still on our first cups of coffee, we call my primary care physician, Dr. Michael Royfe, and tell his nurse that we must get in today. We want independent drug testing. We call a nearby Labcorp office where I have had blood drawn regularly, searching for lab testing experts. I had recently had blood drawn for other lab work. Was that blood still available for additional testing?

"I can assure you this man has never done cocaine," I hear Roger telling a doctor at Labcorp. "He is just floored. What could have triggered a false positive?"

My blood sample at Labcorp already has been destroyed. The doctor tells Roger some medications can cause false positives on the screening, but not on the confirmation. "There is nothing that anybody knows that mimics benzoylecgonine (cocaine) when you confirm it," he says. "It's that unique. Basically you've either taken cocaine or it's the wrong specimen."

I talk several times with Juan Johnson, whom I've known since the American Airlines flight attendant strike six years ago. She has believed in my innocence from my first phone call. "Have you had dental work or a medical procedure using lidocain?" she asks. "It's used as an anesthetic."

Someone at APFA headquarters in Dallas has faxed me the form to request that a different laboratory test my split sample. The form clearly states that I must mail it to AA Medical along with a money order for $98.35 payable to SmithKline Beecham Clinical Lab, where the split will be tested. I'll stop at the post office this afternoon to get a money order and send the authorization by Certified Mail.

We sit in front of the computer and head for a search engine. Roger types in, "Random Drug Testing." One of us talks on the phone; the other works the computer. We're learning the terminology and the testing techniques. A screening test called the EMIT has a high rate of failure. The GC/MS test (gas chromatography/mass spectrometry) is often used for confirmation of results of other techniques because of its accuracy. What tests were used in my case? We wonder.

Another article outlines the lengths of time drugs remain detectable in the body after ingestion. Cocaine remains detectable for 12 to 72 hours, even up to five days with the latest toxicology drug screens now used. That compares to marijuana traces, which remain detectable for two to seven days with casual use and up to 30 days with chronic use. Heroin, or morphine, remains detectable for two to four days.

No matter how a drug is ingested, the body eliminates it through the processes of metabolism and excretion. The major part of the process occurs in the liver, which acts as a filter to cleanse the blood passing through it. Enzymes deactivate the drugs and convert them into less toxic or less active forms, called metabolites.

Internet sites lead us to hair follicle testing, a newer and highly accurate print left behind by drug use that lasts up to 90 days, depending on the length of your hair. Unlike urine, which can be changed by such simple means as drinking large quantities of water, hair is resistant, binding the traces for a long time. Even if you're bald, your body hair can be tested. A 1 1/2 inch length of hair represents three months of collective history of drug exposure. Urine, on the other hand, can only yield about three days of exposure to cocaine. I need to have my hair tested, we agree.

I call Cindy Buff at AA Medical. Her attitude seems cool, very professional. She hears everyday from employees who've had a positive drug test. The first reaction is denial.

"A split has never come back differently than the first," Cindy tells me. "I don't want to give you false hope."

I think I'll be the first. By now, I know I want to see the quantitative results, as opposed to just knowing yes or no, or qualitative. Cindy tells me I need to request the quantitative results in writing. Later, I write that letter and fax it.

Roger places a call to an attorney he met while working on other union business. The attorney asks a few questions and urges hair follicle testing. He wants us to keep in touch.

Dr. Yiannou and my APFA representatives all have encouraged me to call the Employee Assistance Program (EAP). I'm not sure what kind of help is available. But I know I'm beginning to suffer from some extreme stress. I call the Eastern EAP office at New York's LaGuardia and leave a message. I'm impatient. What if I were suicidal?

I pull up my work schedule on my personal computer. Tomorrow, I'm supposed to work a one-day trip, to Dallas and back. I've been removed "sick." Over the next weeks, it becomes an obsession. Do I still exist or have I been eliminated in cyber world? I continue to check from my home. Sick, every day is another sick day, always sick.

Michelle Bertapelle, the flight attendant from the previous evening, checks on me after calling Juan herself. Michelle is worried and at a loss after seeing what happened to me. One by one, Roger and I check in with friends, hoping one of our airline colleagues will perhaps offer that bit of wisdom we need. I sit on the stairs, sobbing, as I talk to a former housemate, fellow flight attendant and friend Cathy Hunt.

"The truth will set you free," she encourages me.

Ironically, Cathy has been "off the line" for nearly a year with a knee injury. A passenger with a steel-toed boot kicked her accidentally when she was working in the aisle. After surgery and a long rehabilitation, she returns to flying next month. I just recently pulled up her flight schedule for July on our computer and mailed it to her home in Florida.

By early afternoon, we're at Dr. Royfe's office. We bend the nurse's ear. I want to know if something is going on that would cause a false positive. My career is on the line. There has been a horrific mistake. She is concerned. She leaves to confer with Dr. Royfe. My medications, though relatively new, wouldn't cause a false positive, according to the doctor. The nurse returns with a lab order for urinalysis. I tell her I also want my blood tested. She balks but eventually comes back with a lab order for urine and blood analysis.

"I need hair follicle testing, too," I tell the nurse.

"We don't do that," she states firmly.

Referral in hand, we head to the SmithKline office on Duke Street in Alexandria so I can give blood and pee. As Roger drives north on U.S. Highway 1, we review in minute detail my activities over the 72-hour period prior to the random drug test.

On Sunday, Roger and I drove his Dodge Ram and a float through the District of Columbia for a parade. It rained and several people jumped in and out of the truck cab. We hung out at a street festival for several hours later in the afternoon, drinking a few beers and enjoying on-and-off sunshine and music. We ate dinner at Mr. Henry's on Pennsylvania Avenue that evening, forced by a sudden downpour from a patio table to a crowded inside table with two older gentlemen who made interesting company. We stopped for a short while at a country western nightclub a few doors down and then went home to bed.

On Monday, we chopped sulfa tablets and gave penicillin shots to Honey. That evening we played cards with Dickie and Denise, our friends who own the farm where we board the horses. Denise cooked dinner and we went home early to watch ABC's "One Life to Live," the soap opera we tape every day.

At the crack of dawn Tuesday, I signed in for my regular trip for the month, work to Dallas, then to Denver and back to Dallas for the night. As a "floating" position this month, I assist serving a meal in first class then move to the main cabin to help finish selling cocktails, serving beverages and a meal and picking up dirty trays. That night, I ate in my hotel room and slept in, going downstairs just in time to catch the free continental breakfast.

I had pizza and Coca-Cola at the gate in Miami while we waited for an airplane. Then we waited for passengers to deplane and the cleaners and caterers to do their jobs before we loaded up Flight 720 for Washington and departed. *There was nothing out of the ordinary. Was I exposed to cocaine while on duty?*

"Are you sure you didn't do drugs and you're not just lying to me?" Roger turns his eyes to me, pushing for the umpteenth time. "Are you sure you didn't go off on Sunday and do a line of coke? Would you put me through all this? I don't want to doubt you but I have to keep asking you."

"I've done some crazy things in my life but drugs is not one of them," I reply, knowing he believes in me but needs the reassurance. "I've never done drugs and I never will. Drugs have never interested me. You know that. I wouldn't even know how to do a line of coke."

It's been less than 24 hours since I was told of my drug test. I've already learned more about cocaine than I knew in my 44 years, thanks to the immediate and exhaustive resources available on the Internet. My previous knowledge was pretty much limited to images portrayed on television and movies. Of all the drugs, why cocaine?

Cocaine is one of the most powerfully addictive drugs of abuse and also one of the most expensive. Users sniff, snort, inject or smoke cocaine. "Crack" is the street name given to cocaine processed from cocaine hydrochloride to a free base for smoking, usually in a pipe, glass tube, plastic bottle or in foil. Its name comes from the cracking sound it makes when being burnt. Smoking allows extremely high doses to reach the brain quickly and brings an intense and immediate, but short-lived high. Injecting the drug brings the risk of transmitting HIV infection if needles are shared.

Colombia is the world's top supplier of cocaine and the United States is the world's top market for the drug, according to a United Nations report. In 1996, according to the National Institute of Drug Abuse, about 1.7 million Americans used cocaine at least once per month. Today, cocaine abuse is epidemic, predominately among persons in their 20s to their 40s.

Because it is such a fast-acting drug and the powerful effects wear off quickly, cocaine is an expensive drug associated with the rich lifestyle enjoyed by rock and film stars and those earning large salaries in the financial markets. Most ordinary drug users regard cocaine as an occasional treat, though there does appear to be some increase in more general use. Cocaine use is appearing in more clubs around the dance scene along with ecstasy and other drugs.

Cocaine is made from the leaves of the coca shrub, which grows in the mountainous regions of Bolivia, Colombia and Peru in South America. Indians who live in the Andes Mountains will chew or suck a wad of leaves pushed into the cheeks.

Cocaine was first extracted from leaves in 1855 and by the 1870s it was a popular stimulant and tonic and used in a range of medicines. Doctors used cocaine as a local anesthetic for eye surgery and in dentistry. Sherlock Holmes, the fictional detective in Arthur Conan Doyle's books, was a regular cocaine user. Coca laced wines were enjoyed by popes and royalty in the 19th century.

Coca-Cola was originally sold as "a valuable brain tonic and cure for all nervous afflictions" and until 1904 contained small quantities of cocaine. At the turn of the century, doctors began to warn of possible dependence and problems with its use.

Roger and I are exhausted but optimistic that the mistake will be discovered and I'll be back to flying within a few weeks. We leave SmithKline and head across the Woodrow Wilson Bridge to the farm to check on our recovering horses.

We can't ride these days, but we muck the stalls and hang out with Dickie and Denise, playing a few rounds of Spades nearly every evening. Dickie, an Italian who can be a hot-tempered, and I usually are partners. He and Denise get into too many scraps if they're paired together.

That evening I receive a telephone message: "Hi. This is Laura Glading, the Northeast Regional Rep for APFA. I'll be handling your case. Give me a call when you can."

4

"People are always blaming their circumstances for what they are. I don't believe in circumstances. The people who get on in this world are the people who get up and look for the circumstances they want, and, if they can't find them, make them."

–George Bernard Shaw

Wednesday, June 23, 1999

ROGER AND I quickly get into a routine, spending every waking moment making telephone calls, searching the Internet for drug testing information, talking to other flight attendants and every medical person we could corner, and sharing the tragic news with our friends and families. There's not time or energy for everything we need to do, every contact we want to make.

We make a good team, Starsky and Hutch. Roger is the blond one. He has Marlboro Man® good looks and fits the part when he's sitting on his horse and smoking a cigarette. If you don't think he's handsome, he'll tell you. People tell him he looks like Val Kilmer with a mustache. He's 5-foot-8. He wears autumn colors, browns and earth tones, with his green eyes. He worries about his age.

We are opposites in almost every way imaginable. I am slightly taller at 5-foot-10, wiry, scrawny some would say, dark thinning hair and blue eyes. I wear reds, black and grays.

Roger is a Libra, an air sign, typically talkative, shining in the social situations he so enjoys. On the opposite end of the Zodiac, I'm an Aries, a fire sign, independent, determined and enthusiastic.

Roger is the dreamer. I'm the practical one. He's got a quick temper and sharp tongue. He says the things other people only think. In sharp contrast, I'm thoughtful, slow to react. I'm determined, even head strong, but believe prudence is a virtue as well. Roger barrels into life like the bull in the China shop. His approach to life is the spaghetti approach. Throw it at the wall and see what sticks.

I'm a planner and list-maker. He cooks. I do laundry and clean up the kitchen after dinner. He's the idea man. I handle the follow-up details. He likes to believe he's in charge. He gets people's attention with incessant teasing and he barks orders. I don't care who's in charge as long as the job gets done. The vanity plate on his Dodge Ram is FLYBOY1; mine is 4FLYBOY.

He lives with a cell phone attached to his ear. I hate talking on the phone. He's opinionated. I'm reserved. He loves to tease. I enjoy the attention of the teasing.

We both grew up in Minnesota a part of large families. He has eight siblings; I have six. The similarities end there. He was inner city; I was a Catholic farm boy. He grew up without a father at home and entered the workforce as a teenager, his degree from the school of hard knocks. I graduated from St. Cloud State University with a degree in communications and political science.

He likes to shop, buying new clothes for every season if he could. I still have shirts in my closet from my college days. To me, the old clothes don't look all that bad.

TODAY, ROGER begins calling lawyers since we realize that this is bigger than either of us. Most are only mildly interested. I call EAP again. Still no person to counsel me.

I call a well-known clinic in Washington, DC. If my medications are a problem, perhaps they've had experience. The pharmacist doesn't have any knowledge of my drugs causing a false positive for cocaine. She has heard of certain drugs interacting to cause false positives for marijuana, but not cocaine. I also talk with an intake coordinator. She says she'll review my case with an attorney. If my medications are related to my drug test, they definitely are interested.

I call an internist I've been seeing about three years. He's on vacation but his nurse calls back. No, she assures me, my medications shouldn't cause a false positive for cocaine. We're playing a big game of phone tag, waiting for people to call us back.

We call our friend Jennifer, in Philadelphia. She's a police officer and also subject to drug testing. She has heard of a list that tells what substances cause false positives. She will check on it. A few days later, she is told the list never existed; she should forget about it and is reprimanded for asking for it.

Finally I reach Laura, my regional union rep, and tell her how upset I am that I'm charged with an infraction that I never committed.

"It doesn't matter to me," she says, referring to my guilt or innocence. "We will get your job back."

Like Cindy Buff, Laura tells me that she's never seen a split sample come back with different results. She hints at the massive and difficult fight I face in overturning a drug test termination. Only a few cases have been overturned and that was before the company had a return-to-work program.

She talks of the "thin ice" agreement with the company that allows a flight attendant to return to the job after the first positive drug test, substance abuse evaluation and necessary education, treatment and follow-up. The returning flight attendant also gives up the right to "grieve" the termination through arbitration channels and gives up all claims against the company. A positive drug test stays on your record permanently and a second positive drug test is career ending. Not all major air carriers offer a second-chance program.

Denial of drug use is always the first reaction when an employee gets a positive test. Laura has heard it before and my story has a familiar ring. I sense her well-founded skepticism. Juan has already talked to Laura and expressed an unwavering support. But I'm frustrated with Laura's lack of enthusiasm.

"It's more than just getting my job back. My integrity is at stake. I don't want to be marked. I want to clear my name. Just accepting the test without correcting the error is like asking me to sell my soul."

Despite the warnings, I hold out hope. I remain optimistic. *My split will come back negative and the nightmare will be short-lived.* The waiting begins. By the end of the week, Roger realizes that one of us should be working to ensure some household income. He reluctantly takes a trip from his crew scheduling.

He doesn't say so but I sense he worries about my mental stability if left home alone. I'm prone to emotional feelings and it's easy to cry. I'm not suicidal but I do have a difficult time focusing. Even simple decisions are difficult. I don't know how to organize my time. Who should I call next? Why haven't I heard back from so and so?

Daily chores, like laundry and picking up the dry cleaning, are overwhelming. I jump every time the phone rings, hopes mixed with fears. My heart is heavy. I feel like I have an iron ball in my gut. When FedEx fails to leave a delivery one morning, I panic. I think I missed an overnight delivery from American Airlines. I call to have the package traced and redelivered. A few hours later, it turns out to be audiotapes that Roger ordered for his union work.

Friday, June 25, 1999

IT'S FRIDAY morning. With no life of my own, I'm giving Roger a ride to work at Baltimore Washington International (BWI) Airport. My drug test is the only thing we talk about. He'll be gone for three days. I call Juan on the cell phone as we cruise down the BW Parkway. She must sense my anxiety.

"You can hang out here," she says. "I'll be home alone all day."

I don't know if she's entirely serious but I immediately take her up on the offer. I need to be somewhere and her house is as good as any. Besides, she smokes and my nicotine consumption has doubled this week. I get directions to her home on the Chesapeake Bay outside Annapolis. I have several errands to take care of and I'll be there in an hour. As I leave the airport, I get scared.

I abandon the errands and go directly to Chesapeake Harbor Drive. I do not collect $200 as I pass GO. Where is my Get Out of Jail Free card? I'm drawing every penalty card from Community Chest. All the other players have property. I have nothing. The board is treacherous. There is no Free Parking for me.

I ring the bell. I hear chimes, but no answer. Juan's black Oldsmobile Aurora, a birthday present from her live-in pilot mate, is parked in the driveway.

Juan is home but on the phone. I know her. I have nowhere to go so I sit on the steps. I take off my muddy boots and set them beside a pot full of wilting plants. I might be here awhile.

The door opens. Thin as a beanpole and nearly as tall as me, she stands there in shorts and blouse, no shoes, no makeup and her hair au natural. She's from Texas (Fort Worth, to be exact) and she laughs that she's not ready to receive visitors as she gives me a badly needed hug. I feel better already.

She distracts me from my pain and anguish with a quick tour of the house, now in Year Three of Renovation. The finished kitchen is huge, well appointed but probably rarely used for cooking. Three cell phones are charging on the counter. Another phone is on the center island and another is on the wall. This woman is a walking advertisement for AT&T.

"Hi Mom," she answers one ringing phone. "Thanks for calling but my birthday isn't until tomorrow. Can I call you back?"

The living room looks out to a finger of the bay. The night before some friends had pulled up to the back deck with their new boat and called. (Juan had left me a message: "I'm with friends on their boat I didn't know they had.")

Downstairs is an entertainment area with wet bar and a Texas-themed powder room. Our shared appreciation of the country western lifestyle has always been a bond.

"Those are my grandfather's," Juan points to a well-worn pair of alligator cowboy boots that will sit in a specially-designed nook. The washer and dryer have been moved upstairs to a new utility area off the bedroom to eliminate wasted steps up and down three floors.

The third level is the master bedroom, with a two-sink master bath and a specially designed shower *without* a drain. The water drains out through the cracks between the tiles on the floor.

"Can you paint?" she asks, pointing at the high ceiling over the stairwell.

"I might need the work," I reply.

The fourth level is the office. Juan's desk is a big table with her laptop computer. One four-drawer file cabinet is full. Other files are lined up in boxes along the wall. I offer to do a day of volunteer union work to help her catch up.

We talk briefly about my case. In her six years of union work, mine is only Juan's second drug testing case. We're learning together. She faxes a few pages of my initial drug testing research to Laura. We're trying to reach Laura, also Elyse Dzialakiewicz, the EAP person in New York whom I've not spoken with yet. Everyone says Elyse is the person who will get me back to flying.

I camp in the kitchen with a cup of coffee, working the crossword puzzle in *The Washington Post,* as Juan returns phone calls. Do her coworkers know how she spends every waking moment thinking union work? To see her work the phone makes me feel I'm home with Roger.

My coworkers have many questions for Juan about the tentative agreement our negotiations team has reached with the company. The vote is two months away. Mass confusion reigns over proposed pay, scheduling and retirement issues. Union members are especially upset that the proposal gives up profit sharing for our work group. There's talk of a petition drive to get a new union. Factions are organizing "Vote No" campaigns. Any other day, I'd be in the middle of the fray. Today, our future contract seems unimportant, almost trivial.

Several hours later, I talk to Laura. She knows I was upset by our last conversation and grants that I have taken more initiative than is typical. She explains that she does indeed care, but above all, her job is to get my job back.

Afterwards, I realize I don't understand the process of what I'm going through at all. I'm at a loss to know what to do next. Mostly, we're waiting to get the results of the split. I'm confident that I will be exonerated.

Eventually, Elyse calls. Juan already has talked to Elyse and pushed for EAP action as quickly as possible. Juan heads down the stairs and leaves me alone to talk to Elyse. I sit on the landing, fighting back the tears. Elyse's voice is calm. She patiently explains the process. I must meet with her in New York for a substance abuse evaluation that will set the course for returning to work.

"But I'm ready to see you right now."

She's emphatic. "We must wait for the split sample results to take that step. Take care of yourself and we'll talk next week," Elyse tries to reassure me. "Everything will be all right."

I'm ready to leave. For the rest of the day, I want a mental escape. I plan to drive the tractor at the horse farm for Dickie, cutting weeds in the fields with a bush hog, and to be close to my horses. Their trust is reassuring to me. I need the peace of open space.

Just as I'm headed for the door, Juan takes a call from Laura. She has learned that AA Medical, after four days, has not received my request to have my split tested. My 72-hour deadline has been missed. I pull the Certified Mail receipts and a copy of the request from my rapidly growing file folder. Juan faxes them to Laura and assures me that my request will be honored since the delay was no fault of my own.

5

"Let the wind blow through your hair while you still have some."

–Dave Weinbaum

Tuesday, June 29, 1999

IT'S BEEN A WEEK, but it seems like a month since my torturous flight home from Miami. Today I receive a certified letter from Dr. James Yiannou of AA Medical in New York reiterating our telephone conversation. My ordeal is real. It's in writing. It's eerie. I've already done everything he tells me to do in the letter. I've called Cindy Buff. I've called Elyse. I opted to have my split sample be tested and paid for it.

In the same mail, I receive a certified letter from Dr. Glenn Scott, a Medical Review Officer, at AA Headquarters near DFW Airport. From NWT Drug Testing in Salt Lake City, the paperwork shows my quantitative level: "Cocaine metabolites as benzoylecgonine 219 ng/ML."

Words I had never heard of before are now a part of my daily vocabulary. Nanograms are a minute measurement, a one billionth of a gram, not an ordinary household measurement. I can't even find "benzoylecgonine" in my Webster's New Collegiate Dictionary but I already know it's a trace element of cocaine.

The National Institute of Drug Abuse (NIDA) established federal guidelines in 1988 for employee drug testing programs. Initial screening under random testing covers five illicit drugs of abuse: marijuana, cocaine, amphetamines, phencyclidine, and opiates. Positives detected by screening are further confirmed. When a drug test is conducted under "reasonable suspicion," additional drugs are added to the screening regime.

Juan has put me in touch with two other flight attendants who have had positive drug tests and went back to work. Their situations and the drugs found in their tests are different. In one case, a testing lab was shut down. In another case, the flight attendant had purchased an over-the-counter medication in Europe that caused a positive test. It helps to share the experience with someone who's been through it. Both encourage me to fight the fight if that's what I believe.

Today, Roger and I tackle the pharmaceutical companies that manufacture the medications I'm on. One of the drugs has been on the market since 1992 and the other two are new. Could they cause a buildup in my liver of some sort and the combination a resulting error in drug testing? Drug company people won't talk to us until we provide our names, address and telephone number.

At Bristol Myers Squib, a representative tells us she has never heard of the drugs in question associated with a positive cocaine test. But she knows of no test data. "It's unlikely but I know of no definite data," she adds.

Same answers at Merck & Co. They suggest we contact the National Institute on Drug Abuse. They point us to our local pharmacist and urge us to check the package inserts. That evening we stop at Rite Aid, two miles away. The pharmacist is empathetic and gives us package inserts. We don't find anything that means anything to us scientifically but then nothing totally rules out our hypothesis either.

I receive a call from Dr. Royfe, my physician. The urinalysis taken six days after my random test is negative for cocaine metabolites. "If my medications caused a false positive a week earlier, wouldn't it show up in this test as well?" we ask ourselves. Whatever the source, it seems not to be ongoing. We're more convinced than ever there is a lab error, specimen problem or mistake in the testing procedure. Otherwise, the sample is not mine.

Bottom line is I need more conclusive evidence. Our Internet search keeps bringing us back to hair follicle testing. Benefits: Adulteration of a hair sample is difficult. Hair offers a longer history of drug use, 90 days versus three days for urine. The courts legally accept hair analysis. Once the drug is in your hair, it stays there, permanently imprinted until your hair is cut off or falls out.

U.S. courts have recognized the value of confirmed drug analysis in hair and have admitted such analysis as evidence, according to one Internet site. "Our experience shows that when one side in a legal dispute of investigation discusses the use of hair drug testing to evaluate the drug use history of defendants, stories change, pleas are entered, or settlement processes begin," states a legal summary from U.S. Drug Testing Laboratories.

I call MecStat Laboratories in Des Plaines, IL, and Psychemedics Corp. in Cambridge, MA. Their people are sympathetic but they only run tests for corporations. They don't test for individuals. Finally, I'm referred to the American Toxicology Institute (ATI) in Las Vegas.

When the woman on the phone realizes I'm not nearby on the Strip and available to walk in for collection, she refers me to several places in the Washington, DC, area that can handle the collection and ship the specimen to the lab for testing. Doreen at B & W Medical Services in Manassas Park, VA, says she can handle the job.

"Can I come in this afternoon?"

"Sure, I'll be here until 5," Doreen replies. Her directions confuse me so I sign on the Yahoo's map-making Internet site and print out driving directions. We're on our way.

B & W is a multipurpose agency that provides contract drug testing services among others. Doreen is a jolly, cheerful type, telling of a man sent to her for hair follicle testing who arrived with a shaved head, free of the dreadlocks that he sported a day earlier.

Doreen is respectful when she sees my "hair situation" and starts the paperwork. For Roger, my receding hairline and male pattern baldness are a source of humor, good-natured teasing I can handle since the rest of my body has more than its fair share. Today, however, is serious.

Doreen comes around her desk, shears in hand. Roger grimaces and turns away. He can't watch. I'm thinking she needs just a few strands. Wrong. She needs enough to fill a small vial. Whack, whack, whack on the back. Whack on the top. Right down to the scalp. Three spots. But it's a good sample, at least

1 1/2 inches long, good enough for a three-month history.

The long 4th of July weekend is coming up. Doreen thinks she may have the results by Friday afternoon and promises to fax them to me as soon as she receives them. We thank her for the help and leave.

Near home on U.S Highway 1, we pass the shopping center where we both get haircuts. Roger makes a quick right turn into the parking lot and says my hair must be fixed. We have pictures for future evidence; now it's time for some vanity.

The stylists in the shop gather around the back of my head, clucking and shaking their heads. "Did you do this to him?" Zefan, my stylist, asks Roger, who grins. The story is too complicated to tell so we give an abbreviated version. Zefan trims closely around the short areas to minimize the visual impact and suggests I come back in three weeks for more repair work.

Wednesday, June 30, 1999

TODAY, lab workers at ATI in Las Vegas receive and log in my hair sample. Within hours the same day, the split sample of my urine finally arrives from the Salt Lake City lab via UPS at the SmithKline Becham lab in Dallas for testing.

Meanwhile, I'm waiting impatiently for the test results.

Friday, July 2, 1999

I'M ON THE PHONE with a friend who's on her way to the hospital with her husband. At 3:24 pm, my fax line rings. If it is Doreen from B & W, her timing is perfect. As I retrieve the fax from my computer, I know, for once, the news was good:

"Requested test: Hair. Drugs Tested For: Cocaine Metabolites (among others). Screening Cutoff 5 ng/10mg. Negative. A negative result indicates that none of the drugs listed above were detected at a concentration greater than their listed cutoff levels."

6

"Nothing is more liberating than to fight for a cause larger than yourself, something that encompasses you but is not defined by your existence alone."

–Sen. John McCain in *Faith of My Fathers*

Saturday, July 3, 1999

OVER THE LONG 4th of July weekend, I'm sure AA Medical is closed. I try not to think about my split sample results. Roger suggests that we drive to National Airport and watch the fireworks.

"You're crazy," I reply. "I don't want to go near the airport."

Later I find out that SmithKline did finish the test on the split sample and report it to AA Medical on July 4 although I don't get the results for four more days. That's three weeks after the original random test was taken.

On Saturday, our veterinarian, Dr. Taylor, stops at the farm for a follow-up with the horses. Honey has made an incredible recovery, which the vet attributes to the fact that she was vaccinated. Unvaccinated horses, she says, usually get much sicker, often having nasty abscesses that require lancing and draining. Her lungs are normal and, even better, she is still carrying a foal, as evidenced by ultrasound.

By the 4th of July weekend, Sizzler, too, is normal. We're holding our breath on Paint and Quinn, our friend Jennifer's horse that shares our field. The incubation for strangles is four to eight days and we know the other horses have been exposed. We're relieved to be off the penicillin routine.

We chat about my drug testing case and Dr. Taylor is interested.

"I've seen horses on the racetrack test positive for cocaine because their trainers have been using," she volunteers. "It's that easily absorbed through their skin."

Tuesday, July 6, 1999

I CALL Cindy Buff at AA Medical. Still no word on my split test. What could be taking so long?

The fax line rings. It's Dr. Royfe's office. My blood workup from last week is back. The tests screened specifically for cocaine and coaethylene, another cocaine byproduct, as well as benzoylecgonine. Reporting limits are 20 ng/ml, even lower than the urinalysis. None detected. The analysis was by GC/MS, the most conclusive of the test processes.

Wednesday, July 7, 1999

MY PERSONAL PHYSICIAN, Dr. Royfe calls about my blood tests. He explains that the drug is removed quickly from the blood by the liver so the window of detection in blood is even shorter than with urine. Blood tests show only that whatever happened with the random test apparently is not still happening.

Later in the morning, our union is holding an informational road show on the tentative agreement for our Washington base. I'm still a member and still

57

looking toward a flying career so I go to the Crystal City hotel and sit quietly in the back. The atmosphere is hostile. People are upset about the proposed agreement. Only a couple of my coworkers have heard about my drug test. I have a difficult time listening; my own dilemma is hard to push out of my mind and it's not a priority here.

Juan pulls me out of the room. She wants me to meet Laura Glading, my union rep who is in town for the meeting. We're waiting in the hall outside the restaurant for lunch orders. It seems like I spend most of my time now waiting for something. I have a great deal of patience but it is stretching thin these days. There's not time or a place for a private discussion with Laura. But at least now I have a face to put with the person who is supposed to represent me.

After four hours of listening to union members and leaders debate over numbers, I can't stand it any longer and leave.

When I get home, I have a message from Cindy Buff about my split. I call to ask her the results. She won't tell me the results over the phone or fax them to me. She says they are being sent to me.

"I can only tell you we've never had a split come back different from the original," she adds. I immediately page Juan and then leave a message for Laura in New York. I want the results and I want them now. I am frustrated and fed up with all this waiting.

That evening I update Denise at the farm. "It was a hint," Denise says about Cindy's comment about the history of splits. "She couldn't tell you on the phone so she was trying."

"It can't be," I say in denial. "There is no reason for me to have a positive test for cocaine."

Thursday, July 8, 1999

AT 9 AM, the phone rings. I'm awake but still in bed. I have a hard time finding a reason to get up. It's Laura with the long-awaited news I haven't been able to get from AA Medical. Laura has been in touch with people at Human Resources who have heard from AA Medical. She has the results, though third hand.

"I'm sorry to be the one to tell you, but the split came up positive," Laura says.

I call Elyse at the Employee Assistance Program in New York. She won't see me until the following week, which will be a month after my original call. We set an appointment and discuss travel arrangements to LaGuardia. The company will fly me to JFK Airport or I can buy my own ticket and fly directly into LaGuardia.

She says she can't see me sooner because she needs the necessary paperwork from other departments before my substance abuse evaluation. To me, this process is bogged down. I want things to happen right now. Hours seem like days; days seem like weeks.

I call the lab in Las Vegas to get more information on the hair testing process. How long will my specimen be saved? How can the negative results be compared to my positive random urinalysis? Record downpours have hit Las Vegas. The person I need is out of the office dealing with flood problems at his home.

My mother has called in recent days but I haven't called her back. I've been waiting for a positive development before I dump the terrible news on my parents, though I have no doubt they will be supportive.

Mom is a registered nurse at a small community hospital in rural Minnesota. She doesn't look or act her age but she should retire and won't. With a daughter and six sons, Mom is not easily surprised. But I think my news blows her away.

I was the serious child of the lot, rarely in trouble as a teenager, an altar boy and member of the church choir. I played drums in my high school band and was an honor student and high achiever, a member of the Spanish and drama clubs. I was editor of my college newspaper and graduated in four years with honors. I love my life; I am practical and cautious by nature. In comparison, my brothers were hellions.

This is not to say I was the perfect child. Once I was left home in charge of my younger brothers. I didn't like their behavior so I locked them in an upstairs room. Unbeknownst to me, they broke out a window and were standing on the roof when my mother drove up to the house. Another time we were playing "doctor" and I prescribed my sister's perfume as pretend medicine. They drank it and got sick.

Nonetheless, growing up on a dairy farm, I knew the meaning of hard work and I willingly took on responsibility. While the East Coast suffers from a disaster drought this summer, the Midwest has more rain than farmers need. Cows are walking in mud up to their udders.

Mom knows there is a mistake without me getting far in my story.

"Medical issues aren't always what they appear to be," she says. "We had an older patient at the hospital that was being checked out for internal bleeding. His bowel movements were black, not like normal. Doctors were checking him out for all kinds of problems but couldn't find anything. Turns out he was eating too many beets. *Beets.* That's all it was."

I laugh. She says I'm always welcome to come home and help out on the farm. There are cows to be milked twice a day and hay to be baled. My brother who is taking over the farm works seven days a week and is barely keeping up.

"I suppose you don't have travel privileges right now, do you?" she asks. "How much would a ticket cost anyway? We could always use your help here."

"Thanks for the offer," I say. "But I need to stay around here to get this resolved as quickly as I can."

"Keep in touch. Don't wait so long to call. Say hi to Roger. I love you, John."

"Love you, too, Mom."

As I head for bed I hear a quiet knocking, banging noise from the air conditioner, which has been working overtime in the blanket of 100-degree heat.

"Just what we need," says Roger, turning up the thermostat to shut it down for a rest.

Friday, July 9, 1999

BY MORNING, the noise from the air conditioner is louder though it's still kicking out cool air. The AC is working on a wing and a prayer and we know it's not going to hold out much longer. I find a repair service in the Yellow Pages. Finally, I locate someone who can get to it today.

After he arrives, he diagnoses a motor problem. We give him a down payment and he orders a motor from the factory. Waiting for one more thing.

Roger takes a four-day trip assignment for tomorrow. He will be getting out of town, doing a double layover in Boston where he'll see the Broadway production of *Rent*. The week before he and coworker had crashed a Rent cast party at their layover hotel. He hopes the AC will be fixed by the time he returns.

Meanwhile, the clothes dryer has joined the AC in appliance heaven, survived only by its washing machine companion. We can't afford another major repair so I'm determined to fix the dryer myself. I pull it out from the wall and start taking panels off. I find nothing. Then again, I don't really know what I'm looking for.

The phone rings. It's a real estate agent wanting to show the house in 30 minutes. I push the dryer back into its space. Roger runs the vacuum cleaner through the house, an exercise we do every time we have a showing. He turns up the AC so it doesn't clank while the house is inspected. An hour later, a prospective buyer sits on the living room sofa, commenting that it seems sort of warm in the house.

"We keep the thermostat high to conserve energy," Roger covers. I try to keep a straight face.

Trying to sell our house in the midst of what's going on seems incongruous. Getting rid of the mortgage makes sense, on one hand. But moving to Tennessee seems a farfetched, ill-timed dream. Or is fate telling us to make opportunities, to look toward change?

We feel like magnets for bad luck. "If it weren't for bad luck, I wouldn't have any luck," Roger likes to say. He's always believed he has bad karma and this week is setting new records.

Denise calls from the farm with more bad news. Her black lab, Bones, will be spending the night at the veterinarian's. He has had a sore paw but it's worse than it appeared. The dog has Lyme disease. He's not ours, but we feel like he is the next best thing to having one of our own.

We do what we're doing best these days: We sit in front of the computer to search for information. Roger logs on and types, "Lyme Disease in Dogs."

"Top 10 of 204,415 matches in your subject search," the screen tells us.

We're good. The Internet has become more essential to our life than the microwave or VCR. I never understood travelers who are on their laptops all the time. Now I know. There is no better way than the Internet to get directions, airline schedules, send a quick note to someone, search for real estate, check on the day's mortgage rates or get some obscure piece of information. The Internet is life. Three of Roger's sisters have computers and we chat with them online several times a week.

Saturday, July 10, 1999

ROGER is gone on a trip and I'm sitting home waiting for the air-conditioner repairman. The promised day for installation has come and gone. I'm calling twice a day. But the factory is swamped with the high demand for parts pushed by sweltering heat that blankets the East Coast. The repairman will be here when the motor arrives or the heat wave breaks, whichever takes longer.

The phone rings. It's Denise.

"I've got news," she says. "Dickie found a dead body in the cornfield."

"You've got to be kidding."

"Johnny," as she affectionately calls me, "I'm serious as a heart attack. Bones would probably have found the body first but you remember he's been sick and not running around like usual."

"Wonders never cease. This I have to see. Makes me feel like my troubles are nothing. I'm leaving shortly. I'll be there soon."

When I arrive, police cars are barricading the road in front of the farm. I have horses on the property so a uniformed officer waves me through. TV news and police helicopters are circling overhead. We feel like we're being watched. I'm paranoid.

Dickie was driving down the road and he noticed a wide swath of corn knocked down in the neighbor's field. He stopped to investigate, figuring some teenagers had driven in and were having parties. Walking in, he saw a man's body lying face down on the ground, pants pulled down to the ankles, a towel over the head, dripping with blood. It appeared to be an "execution style" murder.

In comparison to this man's dilemma, my problems seem minuscule. I'm trying to keep perspective of the big picture of life.

That evening on the television news Dickie is described alternately as a "passing motorist" and a "local farmer." We're amused. He talks quietly on the phone as a newspaper reporter interviews him.

The following day, newspapers report that the victim had been missing for two days and that his girlfriend's blue-gray Ford Expedition also was missing. A month later, the assailant would be found and indicted on charges of first-degree murder, kidnapping, armed robbery and two handgun offenses. Police found the man by following the trail of the victim's debit card. The assailant had loaned out the card and gotten it back, leading police to him at his Washington, DC apartment. I wonder if the Nation's Capitol is still the Murder Capitol of the World?

That evening when the temperature drops below 90 degrees, Denise and I go horseback riding, staying clear of the road and all the police commotion. I am riding Honey for the first time since she was sick in June. At least that worry is over for now, so I think. There's something about being on a horse that makes your troubles feel less threatening. After a good ride, I feel exhilarated and ready to tackle life's problems again.

Sunday, July 11, 1999

THE SUN is setting and I'm at the farm, feeding the horses. I notice Quinn is not his usual curious self. He is standing in the back of the stall, obviously bothered. I check his temperature. It is pushing 104. Not good. His legs are swollen and he's not eating. I head to the house to use the telephone.

I call Jennifer, Quinn's owner in Philadelphia, and leave a message.

I call Dr. Taylor, who advises me to begin treatment right away. She urges a cool sponge bath to help bring down the fever, along with aspirin-like bute.

I remove a bottle of penicillin out of the refrigerator and I fill a syringe. Back in our field, I bring Quinn into a stall, find a big muscle on his rump, jab in the needle and inject the drug. As I've done many times over the past month, I rub the muscle after pulling out the needle. My hands are covered with small splashes of the white drug substance from handling the syringe and touching the treated horse. We don't have a water hookup in this barn. I'll have to wait to wash my hands until I get to the house.

The horse hospice is reopened. Our strangles outbreak is not over yet.

Tuesday, July 13, 1999

THE ATTORNEY who works for APFA, promised by my representative Laura, hasn't called me. And we haven't found another attorney who wants to jump into our drug-testing fray. We've searched the Internet for legal resources. We wrote an e-mail to a Dallas attorney about my case. Roger has visions of a million dollar lawsuit. I have my doubts. The Dallas attorney hasn't responded. Roger is researching referrals through other union members and finally hits on an attorney who has handled some airline cases, though not drug testing.

A day before my trip to New York, we walk into his law office in Old Town Alexandria. The attorney is interested but raises questions we don't have answers to. He wants to see my contract though we try to explain drug testing isn't a negotiated item, therefore it's not covered in the contract. He wants to see the AA Drug Testing Rules, which we haven't obtained. He wants to see the DOT rules, which we don't have. He wants to see the paper trail, which barely exists yet.

We arrive home, reevaluating how big our challenge is. Truth is on my side but that may not be enough. Attorney fees are $200 an hour plus other expenses. We don't have that kind of money and neither do our friends.

I have phone messages from Scott Prentice, my flight service supervisor, and Juan. I ignore Scott for the moment and call Juan. She has already talked to Scott. Flight Service wants me to come in for my termination meeting. If I want Juan there, she won't be available until Friday. I tell her I'm in no rush to be terminated at this point and Friday will be fine. A few minutes later, she calls again. Laura will be in Washington Monday for other business and if I want her there as well, we can wait until then. Sounds good to me.

I never call Scott back.

7

"You don't get what you deserve, you get what you negotiate."

–Advertisement for Chester L. Karrass

Wednesday, July 14, 1999

BEFORE LEAVING for New York in the morning, I call Cindy again about the written results of the split. Though I know the end result, I want to compare the quantitative results with the original specimen. Cindy says that if I don't receive them in the next day's mail, to call and she will FedEx them to me overnight.

Just getting dressed for a business meeting is problematic. For 10 years, I've been dressing for work in the same blue uniform. It requires little planning or thought. White shirt and a choice of three ties. It's easy. Today, I should go casual business but nothing jumps out of the closet at me. I chose khaki pants and a green and black plaid shirt. I also shave off my goatee, which in recent months had been newly allowed in male flight attendant grooming rules. The cleaner cut my image, the better.

Roger and I drive to the Huntington Metro station, park and ride to the airport. I carry a briefcase filled with our research on drug testing and a file full of passenger testimonials from my airline career. I stop at the American Airlines ticket counter to buy a ticket for the trip. No more of these employee-priced tickets for me.

We head for the US Airways Shuttle and check in at the gate. ABC's Sam Donaldson rushes up to the gate to get on the same flight. *Perhaps he might be interested in my story.* Roger, who is with me for emotional support, brings me coffee and a newspaper. I put aside the Life section of *USA Today* because it contains some Web sites with health information that might be useful for future research and we board our flight.

My mind drifts into an abyss as we soar over the clouds. I jump when the seat belt sign comes on, indicating our approach into New York. From the air, New York City looks like a cemetery of competing tombstones. As we taxi into LaGuardia Airport, I put down my newspapers and look out my window at the Welcome to (the Big Apple) New York sign on the berm of Flushing Bay. All those years I worked flights into this airport I never noticed that sign before.

We have an hour before my appointment. We walk outside to have a cigarette and then to the ticket counter area to call Elyse's office. No answer so I leave a message that I'm here.

After 20 minutes and two more phone calls, we find Elyse's assistant at the other end of the ticket counter. She opens the security door and leads the way through the old hangar to administrative offices. Pungent airplane exhaust fumes from below fill our noses. The dingy walls are institutional gray, the floors a patchwork of gray and red carpet, missing entirely in some places, sorely in need of an upgrade. The doors shut with a final, prison-like slam.

We pass a coworker of mine outside the crew operations room. He must wonder what we're doing, dressed for business and carrying a briefcase. He used to fly out of the Washington crew base and he knows Roger. He greets us enthusiastically. I don't know how to explain my presence in a sentence or less so we move on. We'll try to find him after the meeting.

Unlike some companies which have an independent EAP or an EAP run by the union, American's EAP is a part of the AA Medical Department. Seven regional offices around the country offer assistance to the airlines 100,000 employees. While we have 1-800 numbers for everything else and other company EAPs have them, our EAP seems to run on a shoestring budget, almost like an afterthought. Every call I place to New York for help is a long-distance charge.

The door of the American Airlines EAP office is decorated with red, white and blue paper stars. Posters on the walls advertise two AA travel destinations, California and Paris. I ask for the key to the men's room down the hall. As we wait, Roger tries a sugar-free candy from a dish, and then tosses it out.

"Not good," he grimaces.

Elyse walks in, introduces herself and shakes our hands.

"Do you mind if Roger sits in the meeting?" I ask.

"It's up to you, John," she replies.

"You can sit in but you have to keep quiet," I grin to Roger, fully knowing that he would speak his mind given the opportunity.

Elyse is sort of a Bette Midler type, 40-something, a bit harried, a mop of dark wavy hair and glasses that come on and off frequently, brusque but genuine, competent if not overworked. She is the EAP representative for 25,000 American Airlines employees in the Northeast Region; it is just she and a part-time secretary. The office doesn't even have a fax machine. I know she has seen a lot of troubled employees.

We talk about our horses and rodeo. She asks to see pictures, which we haven't brought. The friendly, casual conversation is no consolation to me. This drug test threatens my picture-perfect life. All seems to be crumbling around me.

I'm ready to cry. Elyse reaches across her desk to hand me a box of Kleenex. I gather my composure and tell her a bit of my story.

"I'm horrified and frustrated with how slowly the process is moving. I'm having a hard time holding it altogether at the moment. You can just ask me questions."

"First we'll be doing a substance abuse evaluation and then we'll move from there to getting your job back. We will get you back to work," Elyse assures me. "Try not to worry so much."

Elyse reads from a sheet of paper, asking questions, most I answer quickly and easily. She marks the answers.

"Anyone in your family chemically dependent?"

"One brother who's been sober 20 years."

"How often do you drink or do drugs?"

"I drink maybe once or twice a month. Drugs, never."

"How much do you drink when you drink?"

"One or two beers, three at the most over an entire evening."

"When was the last time you had a drink?"

"I don't remember for certain, but about two or three weeks ago at dinner with Roger, Dickie and Denise. A glass of wine."

"Have you ever missed work or been late because of drinking or doing drugs?"

"No."

"Have you ever woke up in the morning and not remembered what happened the night before?"

"No."

"Do you ever avoid social occasions because of alcohol or drugs?"

"No."

"Do you ever go to a social occasion because of alcohol or drugs?"

"No."

After about 20 questions, she's finished. Later, I learn of the strong addictive correlation between drugs and alcohol, also the genetic connection in addiction.

There is no time or opportunity to share my drug testing research, hair testing results or my attendance or performance records. Today, all that is irrelevant.

Elyse doesn't indicate what her evaluation means or what she has concluded, except that she's sending me to a drug and alcohol educational program, not rehab or therapy.

"A clinic in the Washington, DC area offers a Saturday morning educational class that you need to finish," she says, "then we'll meet again before conditional reinstatement is offered to you."

She gives me a phone number to set up an independent evaluation and our business is concluded. We head to the US Airways Shuttle and our flight lands in Washington at 3:30.

I don't know if Elyse believes in my innocence or not. It probably doesn't matter. By the time I walk in our front door, Elyse has left a message: Kolmac Clinic is expecting my call. She gives me a contact name. The class runs for eight weeks on Saturday mornings in Silver Springs, MD.

"I know it's a long drive for you but it's the best I could find," she says in her message. "I'll be in touch."

I flip out. I can't wait eight weeks to begin the reinstatement process. The fiasco has already turned into a month-long ordeal.

"I could be in and out of rehab in that length of time," I tell her in a return message. "Isn't there somewhere else I could go? I have full days, seven days a week on my hands."

I call Kolmac Clinic and make an appointment for an intake the following afternoon at the clinic's Alexandria office. I'm upset with the delays, the waiting. I need an outlet so I compose a letter to Dr. David McKenas, AA's Chief Medical Review Officer in Dallas:

July 15, 1999

I am writing to ask you to review my random drug testing case and expedite my return to duty. As of today, I have not received the results of my split specimen testing, though I'm told they were sent by regular U.S. Mail on July 6. I know only through third party information that it was positive. Meanwhile, I've been called by my supervisor for a termination meeting.

I have not and would not use illegal drugs and maintain that there is an error somewhere in this process. I have cooperated fully in the process that started 6-16-99 when I was randomly drug tested, then removed from service 6-21-99. Within 24 hours of my removal I went to my primary care physician who ordered lab tests, urinalysis and blood metabolites. Both results were negative. The following week, I submitted to hair follicle testing. The results of the hair follicle testing were also negative and have a window of sensitivity of up to 90 days, well before my random sample. Something is grossly wrong in the urinalysis tests done on 6-16-99 and I continue to seek the answers.

Today I met with Elyse Dzialakiewicz, NE EAP. Her evaluation will be forthcoming to you and I doubt that she will have found a drug abuse problem since I've not used drugs. She has referred me to Kolmac Clinic for an independent evaluation and possible education program. The clinic's program is one hour every Saturday for eight weeks. I have no problem participating in any program but the length of time this would take will mean loss of income and health insurance for at least two more months and create an undue hardship, putting additional strain on my health.

I request an immediate "Return to Duty Drug Test" as provided in the AMR Drug Testing Program, also to continue me on paid sick while I participate in the required clinic programs and until I do return to work.

If you were to review my attendance and performance records for my nine-plus years of service at American Airlines, you would see I am not a likely candidate for any sort of drug abuse.

Thank you for your consideration and attention to my case.

Sincerely,

John C. Ritter

I fax the letter to AA Medical with copies to Juan, Laura and Elyse to keep them abreast of what I'm doing. The Medical Review Officer (MRO) is a key player in drug testing programs. Their duties include understanding how tests were performed, how samples were acquired, how to interpret the results and what courses of action can be taken.

"A positive test result does not automatically identify an employee/applicant as having used drugs in violation of a DOT agency regulation," states 49 CFR 40.33 of the federal law. "Review shall be performed by the MRO prior to the transmission of the results to employer administrative officials. The MRO review shall include review of the chain of custody to ensure that it is complete and sufficient on its face..."

Generally speaking, according to John Osterloh, MD at the Toxicology Laboratory of San Francisco General Hospital, the MRO may choose from several actions; no action, explanation by the employee of conditions leading to the positive test, investigation of medications that may have been prescribed, repeating the test with full explanation of consequences when a second specimen is positive, a change of position within the company, leave of absence, further performance evaluation, resignation, and termination.

In the morning, I call Cindy to check that my letter to Dr. McKenas was received. Cindy is the gatekeeper of information at AA Medical but no one has ever told me her job title. Yes, she says, the letter was given to Dr. McKenas. She tells me Dr. McKenas has reviewed my case and, via her, regrets informing me there is nothing more that can be done. Cindy says he won't be responding in writing because it wouldn't be as expeditious.

Oddly, the results of the split already have been FedExed to me though I hadn't yet called as she requested earlier in the week. I learn from Cindy that the long-awaited split results were not quantitative and that I would have to request in writing, which I do by fax.

Thankfully, Roger bought us a new IBM computer earlier this year. We use it for daily letter writing, playing a few games, which we don't have time for these days, and surfing the Net. I've gotten pretty good at faxing with it.

8

"Nothing has caused more sustained government hot air than the so-called drug war. Now, thanks to the Internet, a cool breeze may be moving in. What we need is increased education and less scare tactics, more treatment and fewer busts. But the leaders of America's drug war are, in a sense, addicted to their get-tough policies."

–Sam Vincent Meddis in *USA Today,* Nov. 24, 1998

Thursday, July 15, 1999

THE OFFICES of Kolmac Clinic are unassuming, located in one of the many historical Old Town row houses on brick-lined King Street. The chairs in a downstairs room suggest it is used for 12-step group meetings. Since I haven't been officially terminated, I offer my company insurance information to the receptionist for payment of the session. Later I will learn the insurance company rejects the claim, even though my company referred me, and I receive a bill for $98.

Counselor Jay Eubanks will conduct the intake for my drug education class. The evaluation is a repeat of yesterday's session with Elyse. Questions about family history, work, alcohol and drug consumption. I am 44 years old. I own a home, a Dodge truck, and a horse trailer with living quarters, have horses and no problems at my job.

Like Elyse, his purpose is not to make a judgment on my action or innocence, or to determine the likelihood of one-time recreational use, but to determine if I had a substance abuse problem. There is no surprise. He concurs: Not addicted.

"From what you're telling me, and I have no reason not to believe you, I don't see an addictive pattern," he says. "It's unusual for someone to reach your age and not to begin to show patterns if there is a substance abuse problem."

He gives me the contact number for the Saturday morning group, shakes my hand and bids me farewell. "Good luck to you," he says.

Once home, I call the number several times, leaving urgent messages, anxious to get in the class the following morning and get one more step underway.

Friday, July 16, 1999

I HEAR from one of the drug education class facilitators late in the evening. She expects the class to be quite full and discourages me from starting immediately.

"I don't mind standing if I have to, just let me get started. I need to get into this class to get back to work."

I also hear from an excited Juan, who had received an odd telephone call from Cindy Buff in AA Medical. The two had shared a friendship in their past. She had seen Juan's name on the bottom of my letter to Dr. McKenas. She and Juan were friends years earlier. Cindy knew Juan was an American Airlines flight attendant now but didn't know she had moved to the

Washington area or that Juan was active in union work. In my conversations with Juan, she hadn't connected Cindy's name to her face since Cindy is married with a new last name.

"It's a small world," Juan says. "We had a good laugh over it."

I wistfully hope my communication and understanding with AA medical will be improved. Perhaps my credibility will be improved.

In the U.S. Mail that day, July 16, I receive Dr. Scott's letter, dated July 6, and the results of the split test. It was postmarked July 12. Earlier in the day I had received the same letter by FedEx. Cindy also calls me about the quantitative results. The first test came to me certified mail; this time, she agrees to fax them directly to my computer: Quantitative level of 202 ng/mL. That's 17 ng different from the original specimen, or 8 percent. It seems a significant difference to me, but it is scientifically acceptable in the world of workplace drug screening.

That night I'm on the computer again, seeking more answers, more opinions. Now I'm consulting online with America's Doctor, getting a chuckle from the response. After outlining the basics of my case, he writes:

"They should make you a poster-boy for a drug free workplace...There is a false positive rate to both (the random and split urinalysis)...There is almost no false negative rate for hair and any time during the time your hair took to grow if you had used ANY it would show up while the urine would be positive for only a few days...most likely the urine screwed up...There are certainly likely to be herbal things somewhere that look like cocaine (itself an herbal compound)...You are cleared by the hair."

ROGER AND I talk of little besides drug testing. Our job is detective work and following up on many dead-end leads. "We need Kay Scarpetta," he says, referring to Patricia Cornwall's fictional forensics investigator from Richmond, VA. "We need an expert toxicologist."

A brief entitled "Urinalysis Drug Tests: Do They Make the Grade?" from the American Journal of Trial

Advocacy suggests problems with certain lab tests used in urinalysis screening and the interpretation of those results in court. False positives in the screening may be the result of a "liver enzyme, which can be created by conditions including kidney tumors, kidney trauma or infection, liver disorders or bladder infections." Positive screens must be confirmed by a second, more conclusive method.

The article also states that neither a judge nor juries are "experts" where scientific evidence is introduced. "The prosecution is required to show that a 'rational basis' exists for the fact finder to conclude that drugs were used," it says. "Introduction of scientific evidence clearly needs in-court expert testimony to assist the trier of fact in interpreting if the prosecution is to rationally prove that an accused used illegal drugs."

Interestingly, the article notes that an herbal tea has been found to contain cocaine in quantities sufficient to elicit detectable levels of the cocaine metabolite, but the Drug Enforcement Agency has had them withdrawn from the U.S. market. The tea is called mate de coca.

Cocaine is an alkaloid of the plant *Erythroxyflon coca.* I wonder if an herbal supplement I had received by mail order in April would be related. I had finished the order, determined the supplement not worth the $29 cost and tossed out the bottle around the time of my drug test. I need to order some more to determine its contents.

WE HAVEN'T gotten our hands on copies of the Department of Transportation drug testing rules or AA's policies. Juan had faxed me some of the policy but the pages were out of order and incomplete. I couldn't tell what I was missing. We've searched the Internet for DOT policies but haven't succeeded in getting useful files. I call APFA headquarters and speak to someone in the health department. The next day I receive the FedEx delivery, a three-ring binder containing the AMR Drug and Alcohol Testing Policy.

By the end of the week, I'm in a state of panic. My work schedule still shows me on the sick list and I'm expecting a paycheck. But my bank hasn't received the automatic deposit. It finally is posted at the bank when I check later. I feel relieved for a few more days. Maybe I won't actually be terminated next week, I hope.

I call a flight attendant friend and coworker who was fired and reinstated six years ago during our flight attendant strike. We've already talked several times. He assures me I won't be terminated without being called in to meet with my supervisor. He walks me through the process as only someone who has gone through it could.

His cousin works in a lab. He's going to see if he can find anything about drug testing that we haven't uncovered. We talk about his bathroom-remodeling project and I suggest a resolution to a problem he's having with the plumbing under the sink.

AT BEDTIME, I watch Roger rummage through the jewelry boxes on top of his bedroom dresser. "Whatever are you looking for?" I ask.

"My worry dolls," he says. "If we ever needed them, it's now."

The six handcrafted colorful, tiny dolls in a basket were a gift from our flight attendant friend, Sharon Price. They probably came from an offbeat witchcraft shop in the French quarter of New Orleans.

Sharon and I attended flight attendant training together, and then lived together in Chicago before I met Roger. She's slightly neurotic and somewhat superstitious. She believes in the Oija board and reads Tarot cards.

Like our friend Cathy, Sharon has been off the line for most of the past year. She suffers from fibromyalgia. She and Cathy know from their experiences the frustrations of dealing with medical issues, not being able to go to work and cutting through bureaucratic red tape.

Roger divides up the worry dolls, handing me three. We silently tell each doll a worry and set them on the bedside table to take up some slack in our lives. I'm thankful to share my worries, though I could use

John Ritter

more than three dolls just myself. I pray that the dolls will be able to return to their basket soon.

9

"Much of the vitality in a friendship lies in the honoring of differences, not simply in the enjoyment of similarities."

–James L.   Fredericks in *Journal of Ecumenical Studies*

Saturday, July 17, 1999

I GIVE IN AGAIN. Roger gets a ride to work at BWI Airport and I'll pick him up when he gets back. With my current employment situation, he believes it's my duty to make his employment situation easier. Today it works. I'll have just an hour to kill before my first drug education class in Silver Spring, MD.

The Beltway is the lifeline of the nation's capitol, connecting people's lives and places. But like a troubled artery, it's frequently clogged. For us, it connects our Virginia home to the Maryland farm where our horses live; it connects our home to the three metropolitan airports where our jobs begin and end. Today, the Beltway connects me to a destination in Silver Spring where I begin the process of returning to my job.

Roger and I spend time together traveling the Capitol Beltway like some people dine together or go to movies. It's quality time for conversation, analysis of the day's current events, music, and mental teasers. Roger passes the time talking on his cell phone, checking in with his fellow union reps, staying in touch with friends and checking for messages on our home voice mail. He uses the phone with the same passion that he smokes, rides his horse and cooks.

Our Beltway experiences also are a frustrating log of our eight years living in Washington. According to a study by the Texas Transportation Institute, traffic congestion in Washington is second only to Los Angeles. Drivers here waste a whopping 76 hours a year in gridlock and road rage increases every year.

Roger and I curse the Wilson Bridge regularly, dreading the day when construction of a wider new bridge begins and traffic worsens before it improves.

The bridge has three lanes; the rest of the Beltway has four. It's like trying to thread a sewing needle with a thick piece of yarn. All the strands don't fit through together.

One day we were stuck in separate vehicles, me a mile ahead of Roger, in the same two-hour traffic jam after a directional sign landed on the Inner Loop. We were on our way home from the farm; I had a trip out of National Airport that evening. I made it with just minutes to spare.

Last year, we were one of the last vehicles to cross into Maryland over the Wilson Bridge, closed for the rest of the afternoon while law enforcement authorities tried to talk down a threatened suicide jump. The resulting rush-hour traffic jam was the worst in Washington history. We were prepared to camp at the farm that night if necessary.

And just this month, we were again in separate vehicles, Roger ahead of me on his way to BWI, as a high-speed chase with gunshots on the bridge ended in a fiery crash a few miles into Maryland. Roger passed the accident moments after it happened; I was stuck for an hour in the snarled traffic. The Beltway again was a parking lot.

Today, we're listening to Celine Dion, crooning the theme song from *Titanic.* Roger envisions my drug-testing saga as a made-for-television movie, his role played by Harrison Ford. I insist I get Tom Cruise to play me. Kathy Bates will be Dr. Royfe's nurse and Sally Field will be a Norma Rae union activist. Cate Blanchett will be Denise. Antonio Banderas will be Dickie. Roger sees a big American Airlines jet landing in Miami as the movie opens. Roger hums the theme song.

I DROP ROGER in front of the USAirways ticket counter and head back to the Beltway. I turn off on Georgia Avenue and head south to Spring Street. I pass Dunkin' Donuts on the right. I want to stop for a sugar fix but don't.

I turn and drive past Kolmac Clinic on the left, checking out available parking. I loop around the block and pull into the lot across the street with 45 minutes before I need to go inside. No one is coming or going from the door under the scaffolding that leads to my class. I push back my seat, stretch out and close my eyes for a short nap. *I don't "deserve" to be here. There must be a greater purpose in my being here, but I haven't figured it out yet.*

Events are out of order. I've been evaluated for drug abuse, determined not addicted and sent to education. But I haven't been fired from my job, yet. According to the American Airlines Drug and Alcohol policy, I should have been terminated first, and then sent to EAP and appropriate education. My schedule shows me being paid from my ample sick bank. According to AA policy, I should have been removed administratively without pay.

I check my watch. Time to go. I'm the first "student" to arrive. I introduce myself to the coordinator and pay the weekly $30 fee. I ask her to send a written note to Elyse that I've enrolled in the class.

"Get the Facts" is a unique, intensive program, probably a more thorough drug education than many health professionals have received. For any participants who may have tried drugs or gotten in a scrap because of alcohol, the education may deter future trouble.

I wait for the coffee to finish brewing, pour a cup and take a seat. The overflow crowd isn't materializing. There are seats to spare. I wonder how drugs or alcohol have touched the lives of others waiting with me. Half the class is black males; only two are women; ages range from early 20s to 50s. I don't know why anyone else is there, except one woman who makes reference to getting her driver's license back.

"It doesn't matter what substance brought you here," Lynn Bailey, the facilitator, tells the class. "But we think it's important for you to understand all of them."

Lynn is a nurse practitioner and a certified addiction nurse with at least 20 years professional and personal experience in substance abuse. Her stories about case histories she's seen and her own family experiences are fascinating. The first hour passes quickly.

We all have a three-ringed binder with our names on it. Every week focuses on a different subject. After eight weeks, we "graduate" and get to take the binder home. I expect it will be a reference guide in my continuing research and exploration of drug testing.

Today's subject is inhalants. Lynn passes out a "pretest" to pique our knowledge and then use our answers as a starting point of discussion.

"I don't expect you to know all the answers," says Lynn. "Availability of chemical substance plays a major role in addicts choosing what they will use. It's not so much the drug of 'choice,' but the drug of 'opportunity' or 'accessibility.' That's why kids get into inhalants, medical professionals get into prescription narcotics and a housewife might abuse alcohol." Lynn gives an example of an office-worker patient who was hooked on sniffing whiteout.

Drug prevalence also depends on the area of the country. Certain cities, like Miami and New York, have access to imports. Predominate drugs in the local culture will be imports like cocaine and heroin. Cities in the midsections of the country, like Salt Lake City, see an abundance of synthetically manufactured drugs, like Eve and Ecstasy, because of a shorter supply of imports.

The class ends with a sobering film highlighting addiction and the high cost of cocaine. One wealthy man used cocaine for years, justifying it as long as he wasn't shooting up. He sold his family artworks to finance the drug. The film also touches on alcohol and nicotine, which is incidentally the nation's number one killing drug. Still, I can't wait to light up a cigarette as soon as I get to my truck after class.

ON THE BELTWAY again, I head to Sterling, VA, to pick up a washer and dryer. Our friends Sandy and Jerry have an extra set in their garage and want to ease one of the week's troubles by giving us the set. The radio is tuned to 98.7 WMZQ, my favorite country western station. Shania Twain is singing about how great it is to be a woman. A news brief interrupts the music.

A private plane piloted by John F. Kennedy Jr. has been missing since last night when he took off from a New Jersey airport and headed for Martha's Vineyard. His wife Carolyn and her sister were passengers. The plane lost radar contact with air traffic controllers around 9:30 pm and its whereabouts is unknown. A crash is assumed and a search has been launched. *Omigod. Another family tragedy.* Robert F. Kennedy's daughter was to be married. She was not yet born when her father was assassinated. Now her wedding is canceled by her cousin's plane crash.

I'm on the toll road leading to Dulles International Airport. I forgot to get directions from Go Yahoo on the computer so I'm trying to decipher Sandy's telephone directions from a scrap of paper. I don't see a road sign I'm looking for, miss a turn and realize 10 minutes later I've gone too far. I back track and follow the road without getting lost again.

Sandy's red pickup truck is parked in front, full of furniture belonging to a friend she is helping move. The house is a comfortable split level with a big backyard. Jerry has a sling shot lying on the patio to chase the squirrels away from the bird feeder.

Sandy has already talked to Roger since I left him curbside at BWI. I can't do much without him knowing it. He must have mentioned I don't always eat when he's not around so she announces I will be staying for lunch. Jerry is recovering from surgery a week ago but he doesn't seem too laid up. I think Sandy has to sit on him to keep him resting. He's been working in the yard. If it were I, I'd be in the lounge chair.

Sandy sets the table and serves up the sizzling steaks Jerry cooked on the grill and twice-baked potatoes. Sandy puts a couple of bottles of salad dressing in the middle of the table and sits down with us. Jerry asks, "Where is the salad?" She cocks her head and shrugs her shoulders.

"Oh," she laughs, "I guess the dressing is just for looks. Jerry claims I'm dizzy."

Both Sandy and Jerry are based at BWI with Roger. The first time I met Sandy was 5 am at a Jacksonville, FL, hotel lobby. We were both there on layovers and Roger had urged me to call her room. We had talked on the phone in the evening and she came down to the lobby to meet me in person before the crew van took me to the airport. She's like that.

We talk about "the job," the unique aspects of working in the airline industry. Sandy and Jerry bid to fly together in July. With him out sick, they may not go to work together until August. Today is the first time I've met Jerry. We talk about his surgery, my first drug education class, the air conditioning breaking, the body found in the cornfield, JFK Jr. in a plane crash and the dog getting sick. The week seems surreal.

They're keeping the washer/dryer in the garage for themselves. We move one set up and one set down. We try to stop Jerry from doing any heavy lifting but he's stubborn and macho. We load the truck, give hugs and thanks.

An hour later, I pass our old neighborhood on Berkshire Court in Alexandria. It's my day to socialize. With no air conditioning at home, I'm in no rush. I pull into a space in front of our old house, next door to friends Jim and Diane, who were our eccentric neighbors for six years. Jim has a complete collection of "Dark Shadows" and feeds our three cats when we're traveling to rodeos. When he worked nights before retirement and we were home, Diane ate dinner with us nearly every night. She doesn't cook much and Roger can make a gourmet meal out of Spam. I've done some Internet research for Diane so I have several pages of printouts to deliver.

They are glued to live television coverage of the JFK Jr. crash search. There is no new news so the networks are running tributes, images of three-year-old John John saluting his father's casket, then as a teenage hunk, *People* magazine's Most Eligible Bachelor and a young New York City publisher with his stunning, classy bride.

Jim and Diane love their game station and want to show me their latest purchase. Last year it was Wheel of Fortune; last month it was an action-adventure spoof. Now they're playing Billiards, three poolrooms with simulated action that is quite real. It's mental diversion for me. I have some beginner's luck and make a few nice shots. It's nearly 5 pm when I leave for home.

I have one more stop. I've ordered my prescriptions refilled for another month (on the Internet) and need to pick them up at Rite Aid. Once I'm terminated, I lose my health insurance. I've been told that under the drug testing rules I'm not eligible to receive COBRA, the self-funded health insurance program unemployed workers can purchase.

I arrive home. A neighbor sees the appliances in the back of my truck. "Are you moving? Did your house sell?" he asks.

"No, but can you help me unload them into the garage?" I reply.

10

"If you believe in your heart that you are right, you must fight with all your might to do it your way. Only dead fish swim with the stream all the time."

–Linda Ellerbee

Sunday, July 18, 1999

I'M UP HALF the night writing a day-by-day chronology of my case for Laura and Juan. I can't sleep. I've never suffered from insomnia before. Of course, I've never been fired from a job before. I've never quit one job before I had another. I've never been a career risk-taker. Before college graduation I had my first newspaper job.

I worked as a journalist for 15 years before responding to a Minneapolis newspaper ad seeking flight attendant applications for American Airlines. The Minnesota winter of 1990 was brutal. I was ready to get out of there. I was unattached and ready for change. I envisioned a life on the beach, briefly, and applied on a lark. American Airlines flew me to Dallas-Fort Worth for an interview, I returned a month later for a medical exam and was offered a job a few days later.

At a farewell party in Minneapolis, my coworkers presented me with a cake decorated in a red, white and blue airplane and a card showing Miss Piggy serving passengers on an airplane. I put my furniture in storage and left for training in Dallas in early April. By June, I was starting life over in Chicago, eager, wet behind the ears, not far off the farm.

Like many others, Roger applied with several major carriers before he landed a flight attendant job. I applied only once and got the job. There wouldn't have been another application for me. I wasn't that motivated. Roger chides me for having a job I was never serious about. I never took the job for granted but it wasn't a job I had worked at getting either.

I survived six weeks of training in safety, medical and service procedures, with written exams almost daily. We called it the Charm School and new-hire trainees probably still do. The women cut their hair and the men buffed their nails. We learned the almost robot-like protocol required for the job–no smoking in uniform, smile and greet, keep the shoes polished and the tie straight. It was more intense than any high school or college experience I had had.

I met Roger back in Minneapolis that first summer I had been away. We were attending a friend's funeral, but that's another story. Roger eventually moved to Chicago and, in 1992, we transferred crew bases at our respective companies and moved to Alexandria, VA.

I'm an above average worker with remarkably few attendance or performance problems in my career. I have 301 hours available in my sick bank. In nine years, I've had five sick calls, the most recent being more than a year ago in April 1998 when I burned my hand on hot gravy while trying to help Dickie cook dinner at the farm. Before that, I was out sick in 1995 when I had surgery for a recurring dislocation in my left shoulder.

I haven't been in my supervisor's office since the new terminal opened at Ronald Reagan Washington

National Airport in 1997. I genuinely like the job, the passengers and my fellow crewmembers. In 1998, I received a Professional Flight Attendant Award, a distinction nominated by our peers. I've handled a fair number of passenger emergencies, an elderly man who had a heart attack and countless sick children. Once, I dealt with a frequent flyer who was having a particularly "bad day" and we eventually returned to the gate to leave the passenger behind at the airport.

Over the years, I've come to appreciate the job. It's not a job you take home with you. If I don't like the passengers on one flight, they're gone in an hour or two and you start over. The variety and flexibility has improved as my seniority has improved. When I travel with the horses, I still fly a full schedule for the month. I just do it in three weeks instead of four.

The job is never regular. The crews, the places and the passengers are always different. I wouldn't call it glamorous but it does provide spontaneous opportunities for fun and a chance to see parts of the country I wouldn't otherwise visit.

A few years ago on New Year's Eve I was in Los Angeles on a layover and called a friend. He was going to a Donna Summer concert at the Hollywood Palladium that night. Would I want to join him? Of course, a disco child of the 70s, I couldn't turn down the invitation.

I've enjoyed Broadway Shows in New York City, Thanksgiving Dinner with a friend in Minneapolis, ice skating in downtown Los Angeles in December, an afternoon at Universal Studios, a tour of Hammersmith Farms in Rhode Island and a sunny winter afternoon on the beach in Acapulco, all on layovers. Just this year on my birthday, I worked a flight to Los Angeles with a two-night layover. Roger went along, we rented a car and spent the day at a rodeo up in Burbank.

I've enjoyed the travel benefits, too, though "space available standby" does require one to be flexible. Roger and I were taking Dickie and Denise to Las Vegas to get married a few years back and were stuck at DFW. The flights to Las Vegas were oversold. When I knew we weren't getting on a flight to Sin City, I grabbed them and announced we were going to

Los Angeles. We boarded a flight and arrived there in the wee hours of the morning to rent a car and drive the distance to the wedding.

Now, I'm about to be fired.

Monday, July 19, 1999

I DRIVE to the Metro Station again. I've been avoiding the crew parking lot at the airport. Though I still have my parking hangtag, I don't feel like a part of the "teAAm" anymore.

The DOT does not require termination with a first positive drug test; American Airlines policy is stricter and does. Other airlines, some which don't have a conditional reinstatement program, handle the first positive test according to their own policies.

At the airport, I punch in the security code and reluctantly go downstairs to operations. I see Juan standing at the end of the hall. She is chatting with crewmembers leaving on their trips. The proposed contract is on everyone's mind. Laura comes around the corner pulling a heavy briefcase on her wheelies. She gives me a hug.

"Hi," she says. "You look handsome today."

I feel like crap.

The atmosphere is casual. Juan calls the process a "formality." *For everyone but me, perhaps. I want someone to pay attention to me.* I feel anxious, like I'm in a fog and no one hears me talking. I'm standing on the railroad tracks and a train is rushing at me. I want to move out of the way but my legs are frozen in place.

Laura is handling another flight attendant's problem today, so she is in and out of my business. I pull Juan into a more private crew rest area.

"I need to talk you before we meet with Scott (Prentice, my supervisor)," I tell her. "I want to review my personnel file, which I've never done in nine years. I have questions."

"Scott is very upset by this," Juan tells me.

I hand Juan and Laura copies of the chronology I compiled the night before. I want to know why a "docs" notation referencing 1992 has appeared on my computer records a week ago and now it has disappeared. "Has someone been fiddling with my records?" I ask. I guess I'm paranoid. Later Scott tells me the record changes were some kind of computer glitch.

Laura tells me she will file my termination grievance, but lacking more evidence it's a long shot, even if the other APFA representatives agree to go forward with the case. If they don't, she personally supports me, she says. In any case, Laura has spoken with an attorney who handles APFA grievance cases and has asked him to contact me.

If I sign the conditional reinstatement, she says, I give up the fight against the company but I can appeal to the DOT. She writes down a name and address and hands it to me. The DOT may not recognize the union in an individual appeal so I would be on my own. Also, the reinstatement is a one-time, limited offer. If I don't take it when it's offered, it won't be available should I lose the grievance route.

It is a terrible choice: Get my job back without clearing my name or face a protracted grievance that likely will fail.

Laura gives me the litigation package covering the testing procedures from the first sample. She has just received it from the company. Basically, it is the company's case against me. It contains chain of custody information on the first specimen, credentials of the Salt Lake City lab, and batch results for the day my specimen was run. The litigation package from the split sample is yet to arrive.

"Not that you believe it or that it helps anything," Laura tells me, "there are people inside the company who believe you."

In Scott's cubicle, I pour through my file. In November 1993 I'm marked "off payroll" for two days. At first I can't figure out what that would be. *Oh,* I laugh to myself, *that was the flight attendant strike.* I hand Scott a misfiled letter that belongs to someone else. He tosses it in the trash can. There are letters from passengers, supervisor reviews and a testimonial from a flight attendant I haven't seen in years. A record that I'm proud of. There are no surprises.

In a half hour, I'm finished. Scott goes to gather up Juan and Laura and we duck into a more private office.

"Do you want me to read this to you?" Scott asks.

"No, it's not necessary."

Today is July 19, exactly four weeks since my fateful flight home from Miami. The letter is dated July 8.

This is a "Final Advisory." My random drug tests indicate I was positive for cocaine metabolites:

Your actions as described above are a direct violation of Rules of Conduct, Rule 33, which states: "Possessing, manufacturing, distributing, dispensing or using a narcotic, barbiturate, mood-ameliorating, tranquilizing drug, either on duty or off duty, except in accordance with medical authorization, is prohibited...

"...you are hereby informed your employment with American Airlines is terminated effective July 19, 1999."

I hand Scott my crewmember ID. It's sad and symbolic.

"I'll keep this in my top drawer for you," he says.

It won't be long if I can help it. Scott doesn't ask for my employee travel card, crew keys or any other company property. He wants to get this over quickly. He hasn't followed the complete termination checklist, but I'm ready to leave.

Juan looks more hopeful than I feel. That must be part of being a union rep, maintaining a sense of optimism. I feel devastated, crushed, kicked in the stomach, angry, even shamed. My gut feels ready to explode. It took a month for me to lose the job, getting it back will certainly take even longer. My once optimistic spirit is growing more cynical.

I've seen first hand how easily the system bogs down with paperwork. Corporate paperwork moves from office to office and desk to desk by snail mail. Unlike flight attendants, gate agents and pilots who are under daily pressure, 24 hours a day, 7 days a week, to keep the airline moving, to be the "On Time Machine," the rest of the company operates 9 to 5. Deadlines have great elasticity. One person out sick for a day or two or on vacation and the paper train screeches to an abrupt halt.

At home, I empty my Roller board suitcase, parked next to my bed for the past month. I stash it in the back of the closet. My denial is over. I won't be flying in the foreseeable future.

I check the computer. I know I no longer exist as an employee so I'm punishing myself. To my surprise, I can still sign into the system but not into my personal record. *"$EMPLOYEE ID INVALID AT THIS TIME$,"* it tells me.

Later in the afternoon, I pick Roger up from work at BWI. He wants to stop to see Mollie McCarthy, his cohort in union work. She and her husband have a home in West Palm Beach but keep a rented house near BWI for their airline jobs. She's wearing her telephone headset as she answers the door. She's setting up a three-way conference call to resolve a flight attendant's scheduling problem. Roger jokingly calls her Leona Helmsly. I'm not sure how he gave her that nickname. They talk several times a day and

Mollie, like all our friends, is upset and worried about me.

Roger and I help ourselves to Pepsis from the refrigerator and give ourselves a self-guided tour of the house. I check out Mollie's yard. I think she could use a gardener and I'm available. We hang out and have bits of conversation between Mollie's phone calls.

"How are you doing?" she asks. "You look relaxed, considering everything. Something good will come out of this tragedy. I don't know what. Maybe you'll become a drug and alcohol counselor."

Oddly, life seems to be moving on, despite my termination. I expected to feel much worse. My senses must be numb.

That evening we're at the farm in Maryland. I wander around the kitchen aimlessly, trying to swat a pesky fly. Dickie is cooking mashed potatoes and gravy with roast beef, one of my favorites. He and Denise are at a loss of what to do or say. We are all numb.

"Johnny," Denise chirps. "We're getting your butt to the unemployment office tomorrow."

THAT NIGHT at home, I show Roger an envelope we've received in the mail from our friend Cathy Hunt. She owns a timber-built home on 15 acres near Hurricane Mills, TN, just down the road from Loretta Lynn's dude ranch. Cathy lives in Naples, FL, with her husband and uses the wooded property as a retreat. Her sister, brothers and parents own adjoining property.

Roger and I have flown into Nashville to meet Cathy at her property several times, once for a big surprise birthday party, another time for a family wedding at Opryland. We missed seeing her in Tennessee for this year's Fan Fair, which was happening at the time I was grounded for my drug test. So Cathy, never to miss a beat, sent us the back stage passes we never used.

"Next year we'll have a blast," she writes in a note.

She knows we're thinking about moving to Tennessee and she's encouraging the thought in her own way. She mailed a current copy of the local Real Estate This Week book, *The Tennessee Magazine* and *Tennessee Homes*. I have already paged through the real estate book and marked some properties that sound interesting with yellow Post Its. Can't hurt to dream a little.

Many have listing prices way beyond our means with acreage and homes that we don't need. But one in particular sounds interesting: "Unique and exciting living area built inside a horse barn. Great room is super for entertaining. Home is attractively remodeled, barn has nine box stalls with center aisle, huge loft, ceiling fan, master down, 6.20 acres, lots to offer."

The list price is $7,000 less than the listing price on our colonial townhouse. It's located just a few miles from the stable in Lebanon where we've overnighted on road trips to rodeos.

"I can't quite picture it," says Roger. "It would be different to live in a barn. You wouldn't have to get dressed to feed the horses in the morning."

The ad inspires us to break from our usual routine of strategizing over drug testing. We can't put the concept of living in a barn out of our minds. We search the Internet for horse farms for sale. My employment future is uncertain so it's hard to think about buying new property. But we need a break and the horse farm dream is in the background, not entirely forgotten.

I set the real estate listings aside and within a few days they are buried under drug testing research papers.

11

"To work on a job where someone complains the pastrami is not hot enough - I think that's good for the soul. You can never have too much humility."

–Miss America 1998 Kate Shindle, waiting tables in New York deli while looking for acting work.

Tuesday, July 20, 1999

EVERY DAY, I try to set priorities. Initially, I figured I only had to swear my innocence, present a case that shows reasonable doubt and sound evidence and the truth would free me. That I would be back to work within weeks. *Fool. Pollyanna.*

Now I need to think survival. I haven't worked in a month but I'm exhausted every night. Whatever pay I was earning as sick is now stopped. I pull out a Virginia Employment Commission informational booklet from my 1993 Strike File. Unemployment never materialized that year since our strike lasted just five days. But I still have the information. I dial the phone. The number is changed and the office has moved. I write down the new location.

I scan the general information. A potential problem catches my eye. "You will be disqualified if the Deputy finds that you quit your job without good cause, or were fired from your job for misconduct in connection with your work," the rules state.

Nothing has been simple. I brace for another fight and another disappointment. I did not do drugs though I was fired for a positive drug test. *How will the Deputy view my case?*

I arrive with apprehension. I expect to see the homeless, the tired and the weary. These folks look surprisingly normal. All ages and races. Men and women. I wouldn't pick them out of a crowd as being unemployed. I stand in the short line. When I get to the information desk, I show my driver's license and give my social security number.

I take the long forms to the table, carefully fill out the blanks and black out the ovals with Number Two lead pencil. The employment history questions go back a long way. I haven't had a lot of employers but they span three decades. I make good guesses at some of the dates. One publisher I worked for no longer exists. I finish and wait for my name to be called.

The gray-haired intake officer is older, obviously good at what he does and courteous. He asks questions and punches information into the computer. I tell him I was fired but that I believe there was a mistake. He assures me that I'll have an opportunity to present my case. He seems to have finished and walks across the office and comes back with a paper in his hand. If my claim is approved, based on my wage history, I'm eligible for the maximum benefit of $230 a week. *Ouch,* I think, *but it's better than nothing right now.*

I will have a "fact finding" interview by telephone. The officer gives me the exact time and date when I can expect the call. If I'm not available, I should call to reschedule.

He tells me that I will need to continue a weekly job search to qualify for benefits, if approved. The weekly filing and reporting system has been upgraded from paper to automated telephone. I call, punch in my social security number and personal ID, and then answer a series of questions. If I don't call, I won't get a check. Any benefit due after the hearing will be retroactive. He advises calling between Sunday night and Tuesday for the best service. He hands me an instruction sheet and I think it looks simple enough.

I have no more questions. The big question is unanswered.

In any case, the experience is not bad, if not a bit humbling. I've had nightmare experiences, on good days, at the IRS, DMV, the passport office and other government service offices. In comparison, this place is remarkably well run and efficient. I'm impressed.

Wednesday, July 20, 1999

LAURA FILES my formal grievance against American Airlines, requesting a hearing and investigation. In format and content, it is a routine, not specific to the nuances of my case. The relief it seeks:

Cease and desist. Immediate reinstatement of flight attendant status. Removal of Final Advisory and any reference to it from all company records and files. Reimbursement of all monies and benefits lost,

129

including, but not limited to retirement credits, all seniorities, vacation, sick time and profit sharing. Any other relief deemed necessary. Conditional reinstatement.

She calls to tell me she done some more research. I am eligible for COBRA, contrary to previous information we had. The policy was reviewed and changed fairly recently, she says.

Good news, except that COBRA will cost money I don't have. About the grievance, Laura is less optimistic.

"The process could take weeks, months, even then you have no assurance that you'll get your job back. An arbitrator doesn't have the jurisdiction to overthrow a DOT rule and a DOT rule is the basis for your termination."

"However," I argue, "it was a company policy, not DOT, that required I be terminated. DOT rules *do not* require termination after one positive drug test."

I tell Laura I haven't heard from the APFA attorney.

"He's been in court this week. I'll ask him again to call you," she says.

"Hasn't any other flight attendant ever had this happen?" I ask Laura.

"Not that I know of," she answers.

I start making phone calls to get temporary work, beginning with a few people I know that have their own businesses. I feel caught between the proverbial rock and hard place. I don't want to make a long-term commitment to a new job, but I need to get back to work. Also, I'm not sure how to present to a potential employer my sudden departure from my airline job.

I dust off my resume, not updated for 10 years. *Employment Objective:* Survival. *Job Experience:* 15 years as a journalist, nine years as a flight attendant and a month as a drug test researcher.

When I was in my 20s, I got part-time work from a temporary agency back in St. Paul so I know there are a variety of jobs out there. One year at Christmas I worked as a Santa Claus at a shopping mall. I hated the parents who forced their kids to sit on my lap for pictures. Their dirty diapers stunk and the babies cried. Another time I was survey-taker at a new car show.

I call one local agency. They have a lot of college students with them this summer and don't need help. Next I call Express Personnel in Springfield. I make an appointment for the following Monday to test my office skills and fill out an application.

Dickie has agreed let me work off my horse board while I'm unemployed. It doesn't pay my bills, but at least reduces my expenses. Every free hour I'm not working on my case, I try to be at the farm. I'm painting the fences around the property and helping out with whatever else needs to be done.

AFTER WEEKS of trying, I finally get through to Kathleen Rhode, the lab manager at ATI where my hair follicle testing was done. The news is mixed. She tells me my sample will be discarded after 30 days unless I request in writing that it be saved for a year.

"In court, a hair follicle test will not refute urinalysis," she says. "One time use will not, or may not, show up in hair. Hair will show repeated use over

90 days, but not necessarily for one day. For an infrequent user, once might not show up in the hair. It detects regular use over a period of time."

On the other hand, she points out, cocaine is extremely easily absorbed into the body.

"It can be slipped into a drink or food," she says. "It is as easily absorbed through the skin on your hands as in the nose or mouth. There is no way to know if you picked it up unknowingly. Children who live in crack houses will test for cocaine because of household exposure."

The more we know, the less we know. *Where is the mistake in my case?* Each time I think we are about to take a step or two forward, we are thrown back five or six. The effort before use grows larger rather than more focused. Now we add involuntary exposure to the list of possibilities, already including medication complications, testing error and sample adulteration. We don't know the answer and we may never know.

Thursday, July 22, 1999

I PLACE A CALL to Elyse in New York. I've started my drug education class and I've been terminated officially. I need to see her again to get back to work. When she calls back, I tell her I want to make the follow-up appointment to see her.

She refuses to see me this week or next, despite my pleadings. She schedules another appointment in New York for Monday, August 9. That's three weeks away. More time missed from work. More stress. More waiting.

THE PHONE RINGS. It's Michelle Bertapelle. As long as I've known her, we've never talked on the phone before. Now we talk about once a week. She's been connected to this ordeal with me from the beginning. She's a welcome link to my coworkers and provides a sounding board for my frustrations.

She and Pete recently ran into each other at DFW Airport. They're not comfortable talking about my case with others, feeling that I should be the one to tell my story to my coworkers. They don't want to fan jump seat rumors. With other flight attendants in the conversation, Pete asks Michelle about their "buddy," meaning me in their secret code. She tells him I have been terminated officially but I am getting along "okay."

Friday, July 23, 1999

"WHY ARE you in such a foul mood tonight?" Roger asks as I sit silently in bed. Bad moods are rare for me and this is obvious. Monica, one of our cross-eyed Siamese cats, crawls up on my chest, snuggles under my chin and purrs. She seems to sense my depression and wants to cheer me up.

It's the end of the month, I tell Roger. I checked to see if my final paycheck had been deposited in my bank. It was only $127. I can't figure out why the paycheck is so small. The end of my financial rope came more quickly that I expected. The noose is tight around my neck. I'm worried.

Besides losing my income, I have out of pocket expenses for my class and for hair testing. I have my share of the mortgage due, credit card bills, utility bills and a high veterinary bill, not to mention food, gas and household expenses. The telephone bill has skyrocketed to more than $300 a month with all the recent long distance calls. I've noticed the tires on my truck need to be replaced. I need an eye examination and my contact lenses are getting fuzzy.

Our budget is based on two incomes and my half has disintegrated. We've always lived close to the edge of our means. I'm about ready to fall over the edge and I fear I'm pulling Roger with me.

The financial security I've known my adult life has been pulled from under me, like a throw rug on a slippery bathroom floor. I think of the scraggly bearded veteran I see on the Beltway entrance ramp. He holds a sign, "Help Me. Unemployed. God Bless." *Is that me next month? Sleeping under a bridge?*

Unemployment benefits, if I get them, are a drop in the bucket. I have $1,000 in an old IRA account I can bust. It would meet a month of expenses, then what? My credit union savings account won't go far but it will cover my credit union loan payments for a month or two.

"Stop worrying," Roger says. "You can't do anything until Monday. You need to call and find out what happened to your paycheck."

A parachute to keep me afloat another month arrives by overnight delivery on Saturday. It is a final settlement check from American Airlines covering my last working month of June, plus all my earned vacation time. Rather than an automatic deposit, a real check was cut. I can pay another month of bills.

I can keep the wolves away from the door for a few more weeks. But financial survival needs to take a higher priority than the ideological pursuit of righting my wrong, I vow to myself. I sleep, but I have no dreams.

12

"The shoe that fits one person pinches another. There is no recipe for living that fits all cases."

–C.G. Jung

Saturday, July 24, 1999

THE HERBAL SUPPLEMENT I had been taking before my drug test arrives in the mail from National Marketing Group, Inc. in Fort Lauderdale. It is called Vilagra (yes, I'm embarrassed to say, a mail order knockoff of the well-known real drug). Not that I had a problem, but at the time I thought it might not hurt.

The directions on the label recommend two capsules, twice a day, preferably on an empty stomach. Do not exceed eight capsules on any given day. Spread dosages by four to eight hours. I know I took less than the recommended amount since the first order lasted 2 1/2 months.

Its ingredients are listed as Maca, tribulus terrestris, androstenedione, niacin and bioperiene, none would appear to be related to the cocaine herb I read about. Still, I nervously put the supplement away.

IT'S EARLY SATURDAY. I drive Roger to BWI and I'm back the Kolmac Clinic in Silver Spring for my second week of drug and alcohol education. This week's topic is over-the-counter medications, narcotics and prescription drugs.

Interestingly, many cough syrups, available to minors in the drug store, contain a high amount of alcohol. Alcohol is an emulsifier, meaning that it keeps all the ingredients mixed together so they don't separate into layers. Some over-the-counter medications may trigger drug screens so it's important to check the labels. Codeine in prescription cough suppressant or antidiarrheal, for example, will test positive for opiates.

Class is out and I head to Sandy and Jerry's home in Sterling, VA. I used their moving "dolly" when I moved the washer and dryer so I'm returning it. Also, they need "trip sheets" before bidding their work schedule for next month. Roger had extra copies and thought I could deliver them.

Jerry is putting new carpet in the dining room and Sandy is painting. Earlier, she was cooking leftover candle wax on the kitchen stove. The pot started on fire. Smoke filled most of the house. The walls and ceilings need repainting. They're glad to see me and take a break from their painting. Today she is serving shrimp cocktail for lunch. I'm still waiting for the salad.

Next I head back to Maryland to check on Quinn, who is getting better, and to do some farm work for Dickie. Sitting in the kitchen, I draw up a syringe of penicillin for that evening's shot. Inspired by the morning's discussion on drug labels, I study the bottle. Bells ring in my head: *Sterile Penicillin G Procaine Aqueous Suspension.*

This is not just penicillin. Each mL contains 20 mg of procaine hydrochloride, which is an anesthetic. That helps numb the area for the injection. It is a restricted use drug for livestock, not for human use.

Procaine is certainly related to Novocain, lidocain and, perhaps, cocaine. I do know that cocaine is used as an anesthetic for certain types of surgery involving the nose, throat, larynx and lower respiratory passages. Roger remembers once having cocaine after a car accident when he had an uncontrollable bloody nose.

I've been exposed to Procaine almost daily since early in June, first giving shots to Honey, then Sizzler and now Quinn. Every time I fill the syringe, there is spillage on my hands. Once I give the injection, I rub the horse's hide to stimulate the muscle. There is usually residue left and then I have to discard the needle and clean up the syringe.

I remember an article I read about false positives in drug testing. A drug is reported to be present but is not actually present due to operator error or it may be due to the presence of a substance mistakenly identified as the drug being analyzed.

The next evening, Roger is home cooking dinner. I tell him of my suspicion about procaine. "You might have something there," he says. We go back to the computer for more research. We learn a lot but don't find what we're looking for. Procaine penicillin has a long duration of action and is used to treat sexually transmitted diseases as well as other illnesses caused by penicillin-sensitive organisms.

When Dr. Taylor, our vet, calls to check on Quinn's recovery, Roger hits her with our latest theory. "Remember our discussion about racetrack horses coming up positive to cocaine?" he asks. "I was focusing on the sulfa tabs. But the penicillin actually contains Procaine."

"Yes, that's correct," she says.

"Could the positive tests be related to procaine?" he asks.

"Highly unlikely," replies Dr. Taylor. "No. But I see where you're headed. It's a good theory actually."

We weren't convinced. That night I draft another letter to Dr. McKenas, outlining my latest information. I fax it to Laura for review before I mail to AA Medical. Later I learn that she has reviewed the issues with doctors at AA Medical. One of the doctors on staff has horses and they determine my theory is unfounded. They insist benzoylecgonine, cocaine's trace element, cannot be mimicked by *anything*.

13

"Never be afraid to try something new. Remember the Ark was built by amateurs and the Titanic by professionals."

—Unknown

Monday, July 26, 1999

IT'S MONDAY. Things seem to happen on Mondays. It is my appointment with Express Personnel. The interview fulfills one of the required weekly job contacts I need to make before receiving unemployment benefits, if I qualify. Besides, I hope it will yield temporary employment that would pay more than unemployment. I trek the Beltway to Springfield and pull into the strip mall parking lot. I feel a nervous flutter in my stomach.

These folks are friendly. I start filling out the application as the three people in the office chat with me. When they hear I was an airline employee, they check with an airline charter company at Dulles

International Airport that occasionally has ticketing positions open. None right now but maybe at the end of the month.

I answer questions about my computer skills, typing speed and equipment operation. I've driven farm tractors and my father's combine. I know several desktop publishing computer programs and have worked in customer service. When I get to the question about leaving my previous employment, I pause. I skip the question and move on. In the paperwork I find their drug and alcohol testing policy. I chuckle to myself. *Right up my alley!*

I complete the forms and hand them in. I tell them that I was terminated because of a positive drug test, to cocaine, but that I'm fighting to get the job back, to find the mistake and to clear my name.

"I abhor drugs and don't have a problem with drug testing in the workplace," I say. "I plan to get that job back but I need work to hold me over for awhile. I don't know how long it will be before I go back."

They seem to understand and like me. I think I'll get work from these folks.

I complete the skills tests consisting of long math, alphabetizing and spelling. It takes about an hour and I'm done. Celeste, the staffing manager, briefs me on how the agency works. We talk about the kinds of jobs that would fit me and pay. My expectations are unreasonably high. I will have to compromise.

ROGER CONTINUES to work his own union resources. Among his contacts is Lisa Wilds, the head of the workplace drug-testing program at USAirways. He goes through the story and tells her that he's not looking for a professional opinion as much as he seeks guidance.

"It's unlikely that a specimen will test positive if it weren't positive," she says. "I can't think of any drug that could have triggered a false positive."

Referred by another flight attendant who has worked in the field of drug abuse, Roger is talking to Dr. Bob Kokowsky, head of a testing lab in Catonsville, MD. We wait to reach him in the evening since he works 5:30 to midnight shifts.

"My name is Roger Holmin and I'm with the Association of Flight Attendants," he says.

"I'm working on a case of a flight attendant who tested positive in a random urinalysis. It was not actually cocaine, it was a trace element, benzoylecgonine, as you know."

"Couldn't you give me an easier one, like opiates, so I could answer with poppy seeds?" replies the doctor, inferring that some other drugs, including marijuana, are less complicated.

"I assure you this flight attendant did not do drugs. Can you give me your take on it?"

"My bet would be a screw up in the lab or chain of custody," says Dr. Kokowsky. "However, there are still things that can happen."

Roger discusses the litigation package, the labels on the two specimens and asks if he would review the information for us.

"Yes," he says. "I would be happy to."

They discuss the lack of signature by the courier. Dr. Kokowsky says a signature is not required by the courier that handles the specimen between collection and receipt at the lab. But the labels I initialized at collection should be a part of the chain of custody package.

Dr. Kokowosky brings up the possibility of "dirty money," meaning dollar bills literally contaminated with drug residue, not money earned from an illegal drug sale, and the widespread prevalence of illegal drugs in our society today.

"You mean to tell me if a passenger rolled up a dollar bill from his pocket and snorted cocaine in the airplane lav, then handed it to me for a Bloody Mary, that would be enough to expose me to cocaine?" Roger asks incredulously.

"Yes, that's right," Dr. Kokowsky says. "Remember your flight attendant's positive test levels were not that high. Yes, I believe it could be a possibility."

Roger is shocked. He imagines flight attendants going to work wearing latex gloves while they collect money from passengers for cocktails and movie headsets.

When I get home, Roger pulls the dollar bill trick on me. "What would a drug user snort cocaine with?" he asks.

"A drinking straw," I suggest.

"No," he says. "Think what you always have on you that's handy. A dollar bill."

Roger pulls a bill out of his pocket, rolls it up tightly and puts it to his nose. Then he hands me the money. I'm amazed.

"Either flight attendants need to protect themselves at work or the Department of Transportation needs to raise their screening levels for cocaine if it's that easily absorbed into the body," I say.

SO I'M NOT surprised when I later read about a study in England that found 99 percent of the bank notes in London were contaminated by cocaine. Of 500 notes at the Bank of England's returned note centre tested at Mass Spec Analytical, just four were clean. Nearly one in 20 were found to be tainted with high levels of cocaine, suggesting they had been in close contact with the illegal drug.

The findings, commissioned by BBC Newsroom South-East, suggest that almost every bank note in London contains traces of cocaine. The results do not suggest that most notes are used to snort cocaine, rather than most are contaminated by currency handled by dealers or users.

Scientists also found that four percent contained traces of ecstasy, with one in 100 notes testing positive for high levels of both cocaine and ecstasy. Cocaine is believed to be spread on to notes by bank sorting machines, transfer by human hands that have handled the drug and by dirty notes rubbing against clean notes while sorted.

"Once you've taken a snort, the compounds will be in the oils of your skin and they'll get transferred to the notes you handle," says Joe Revy of Mass Spec Analytical. "That's the main way in which the cocaine gets on to the notes. When you test notes that have been used directly to snort cocaine, you get a great big reading and the machine takes quite while to settle down. You don't miss the difference."

WE GO BACK to scrutinize the litigation package from the first test. Somewhere in these 100-plus pages of information there must a clue as to what happened to my test.

We study the chain of custody information. According to our research on Department of Transportation testing procedures, we should have copies of the seals I initialed when my random sample was done. Those seals are not part of the package. This vital piece of information is missing. We question the two days from when my sample was taken until it arrived at the lab. There is no signature from UPS, but we're told that is standard practice.

We read the testing procedures. The screening done on June 18 reveals positive results for cocaine metabolites. "To be considered presumptive positive, the drug or metabolite concentration must be equal to or greater than the screening cutoffs established by the Department of Health and Human Services," states the laboratory procedure.

The screening level for cocaine metabolites is 300 ng/ml.

The confirmation test conducted on June 19 identified my specimen at a level of 219 ng/ml. That level is greater than 150 ng/ml, the minimum quantitative test required to call a specimen positive for cocaine, but less than the screening cutoff.

We are confused. If the lab results for the confirmation are correct at 219, how did the specimen pass the screening level that has a cutoff of 300? To our untrained eye, it appears the specimen shouldn't have been considered positive beyond the screening. Is there an error in the screening level test? Is this a discrepancy between facts? One of the tests must be in error.

The document goes on to explain the different state-of-the-art tests and their reliability. "Specimens are reported as positive for a drug only if they meet three criteria," concludes the report. "They must have a valid chain-of-custody record, the immunoassay must be positive for the drug, and the drug's presence in the urine specimen must be confirmed by GC/MS. Specimens not meeting all three of these requirements are reported as negative."

The document also includes the calibration records for the testing equipment and confirmation batch reports from my specimen. Besides the seven control samples, four other specimens were tested with mine. Mine was 219 ng/ml; one had a level of 107 and was considered negative; one was 665 for positive; one was 1383 for positive; another shows a low amount, not measured, for negative.

Saturday, July 31, 1999

THIS WEEK'S drug class focuses on family, nature vs. nurture, and the interaction between family, religion, peers and media. The family rules in addiction: Don't talk. Don't trust. Don't feel.

"Everyone whose life touches the alcoholic or addict is in one way or another affected by his disease," Lynn says. "They usually experience the alcoholic or addict's suffering as well as their own."

The roles in an addictive family: Chemically dependent, chief enabler, scapegoat, family hero, lost child and mascot.

"The roles aren't just at home," Lynn tells the class. "They go to work and everywhere else with you."

14

"The only way you can truly control how you're seen is by being honest all the time."

–Tom Hanks in *Interview Magazine*

Monday, August 2, 1999

I SHOULDN'T BE surprised. At exactly 10:40 am on Monday morning, the Deputy Commissioner for Virginia Employment calls for my unemployment case hearing. It's the first phone call I haven't sat waiting around for. It's the only institution in my life these days that seems to run with any resemblance of a schedule.

Ms. Willner is professional and to the point. She wants facts, not complicated by speculation. I hear her computer keyboard clicking in the background as we talk. I tell her that my drug test was positive but that it is an error. I tell her I had my hair tested to prove my innocence and that I've filed a grievance to get my job back. She asks questions, I answer. She's careful to not offer me any reaction to what I'm saying. Her impartial attitude both impresses and frustrates me.

As we finish, I offer to fax her any materials to support my testimony. She asks how many pages. Three for the chronology, one for the chain of custody document, three pages of my personal test results for drugs, including the hair follicle testing, and one for the termination grievance filed by my union. That would be fine, she says, giving me her fax number. I still hold little hope that a government agency would rule in favor of the little person. I'm just not optimistic.

"How long before there is a decision?" I ask. "What are my chances?"

Ms. Willner can't offer her opinion at this time. She tells me the company will be asked in writing to respond to my claim. A decision will be rendered by the end of next week based on the information available at that time, she says.

Since I don't have a scanner on our computer I can only fax documents that originate on the computer. I compile the pages to take them to a local store for faxing.

While I was on the phone with the Deputy Commissioner, Express Personnel has called. They have a potential job for me.

"It's a customer service position with a bottled water company," says Lindsay. "You'd be answering the phones and taking orders for water delivery. The office is very casual, shorts and T-shirts."

"So long as I'm not soliciting or bill collecting, I can handle it."

"Can you go there this afternoon?"

"Sure, you can tell them I'll be there by 2 o'clock."

I can't afford to be picky about work. I pull up driving directions on Go Yahoo. It's only eight miles away in Lorton. I shower and dress casually in black jeans and a Polo shirt. The shorts will have to wait until I see the other workers. On my way, I stop to send my fax to the Deputy Commissioner.

At 1 pm, I pull up in front of Aqua Cool. The warehouse and adjoining office building are painted robin's egg blue. Several blue delivery trucks are parked in the area. I circle the building once before I find an empty parking space.

A young woman in the front office wearing a white tank top and Daisy Duke denim shorts directs me to the customer service manager in the back. She's on the phone. I stand aside and she directs me to pull up a chair. She briefs me between calls. This woman must be on a lot of caffeine, considering the speed she moves around the office and talks.

Three desks on either side of her have computers and telephones. On the other side of the room are a copy machine, fax machine and a row of file cabinets. A water cooler in the corner is evidence that employees use the product the company sells.

Rita has been on the job three months. Two others, also from the agency, just started this morning. One is not back from lunch yet and Rita promises to straighten him out on break rules.

"You'll be answering the phones and helping resolve customer problems," she says between constant interruptions. "Can you stay this afternoon?"

"Sure, at least until 5."

"Then you can watch Karen over there and by tomorrow morning, we'll have you on the phone. We need the help."

I pull up next to Karen, who briefs me between the steady rings of the telephone. This is the delivery schedule. A new computer system was installed this summer. The company recently bought out another water business and its customers have new account numbers. At 5 pm, I feel barely oriented to the business, but I promise to be back at 8 in the morning.

MARY WHARTON, our real estate agent, has called several times in recent weeks. We haven't told her I lost my job or that our enthusiasm for selling the house has waned. Roger suggests taking it off the market. I say no. Not yet anyway. At least let the contract run until it expires in September.

"If the house sells, we'll have money to finance my fight to get my job back, to hold us over," I suggest only half in jest. "I don't want you to give up on the dream of having a horse farm in Tennessee and I will be going back to work eventually."

"But when?" he asks.

The timing sucks. The numbers make sense. The sale of the house should net enough to give us a down payment on a property with acreage. Without state income taxes, lower property taxes, no personal property taxes and our own facilities for our horses, we would reduce our expenses by more than $1,000 a month. We're fools for staying in Virginia.

Roger returns Mary's call. She wants to talk about new marketing strategy. She suggests lowering our listing price to attract more traffic. She thinks we're asking too much. *Story of my life.*

"I want to sell the house, not give it away," Roger tells her. "Bring us an offer and we'll talk about lowering the price. We haven't had one offer yet."

15

"Nothin's better than a cool drink of water – but too much can give you a bellyache."

–Texas Bix Bender in *A Cowboy's Guide to Life*

Tuesday, August 3, 1999

SO I ENTER the 8-to-5 workday world, the rat race from my pre-airline days. I arrive early at 7:30, in time to find a vacant desk for the day, get a cup of coffee, ready to answer the phone. Not everyone is here yet and chaos already reigns.

"Good morning. Aqua Cool. This is John. How can I help you?"

One of my first customers is a woman who's been trying to get through for weeks. She doesn't care that I'm new at the job and may not be able to help her. She's just glad to finally have reached a real person.

I soon discover the unavailable button. It's a sanity saver. I can push it to stop incoming calls from rolling over to me when I need to take a bathroom break. I also can use the button once I take a call to stop the second line on my desk from ringing.

Me on the telephone. The image makes me think of the "I Love Lucy" episode when Lucy Ricardo took a job as a switchboard operator and couldn't keep all the lines going to the right offices.

There is an unidentified place called "Five-0" where workers send calls and page someone at an undetermined location. If someone pages me to pick up a 5-0, I'm not sure how I'll land that caller on my line before I disconnect him or her. My first day I take 40 or 50 calls, keeping a log of every customer, writing down account numbers in case I delete them from the computer before I resolve their problems. I know how to put in an order for more bottled water but every other call presents a new problem.

"I didn't get my July bill yet."

"I need an invoice from May before I can pay that bill."

"The driver didn't pick up my empties this morning."

"I canceled my service a month ago and no one has come to pick up my cooler yet."

"I need to order coffee supplies."

"When is my next delivery date?"

"Someone promised me water last week and it still isn't here. We're dying of thirst."

I always thought the traveling public was needy and asked a lot of questions. People with empty water coolers in their homes and businesses aren't a very happy lot either, especially when the heat and humidity hits nearly 100 degrees every day. You can only tell them the water is on its way so many times.

I finesse when I don't have the answers and quickly learn who does what in the office, or rather, who doesn't do much. One person absent in the office apparently handles invoices and no one else knows his job. It's called job security. He is out sick and may not be back for weeks, maybe months.

The names of several drivers keep popping up in customer complaints. Either their routes are troublesome or they routinely forget certain deliveries. Several drivers are out sick and others are doubled up on deliveries. Some are two or three days behind schedule.

Every morning, we get driver route sheets telling what stops are scheduled. If it's ordered and doesn't get there, I don't know why not or when it will, if ever. Within a few days, I learn how to page drivers to check on specific deliveries and how to print an invoice from the old computer system. I can fax and I can copy. In a couple of days in the water business, I quickly graduated from the dog paddle to the breaststroke.

I've also cut way back on my smoking. The five or six of us in the customer service pool can't all be gone from the phone at the same time or for long.

The second day, Roger takes a call at home from Express Personnel.

"Yes, John is on the job where you sent him," Roger says.

"Someone over there is giving out our fax number and we're getting water orders," Lindsay tells Roger. "It has to stop. Will you give John the message when he gets home?"

Roger can't control his amusement so he calls me right away. I think he has to be joking. Knowing my difficulty with telephones, only he could come up with such an appropriate prank. Once I'm convinced he's not pulling my leg, I figure out the culprit, another temp from the agency, is sitting across the room from me. We have a good laugh.

I catch on quickly and don't have to be told the same thing twice. But office procedures and management change almost daily. A route driver from last week is now the general manager. Last week's general manager is now out on a route making deliveries. Even workers who've been there awhile seem frustrated.

During a cigarette break, I'm talking to Karen. She's been there seven years and is one of the few workers who wear business attire to the office. She says you never know when someone might walk in and offer you the job of a lifetime. But we don't get much street traffic in this remote location. Karen warns me the phone calls this week are nothing compared to the week customers receive their bills. I can't wait.

I take 15-minute lunch breaks and stay past 5 when Rita needs help on an extra project. I'm used to working odd hours and this is nothing. Every hour is another buck. I'm worried about where my finances are heading. Even a low-paying job is better than no job.

Within a few days, I'm more anxious than ever to return to my flight attendant job. Even working evenings, weekends and some holidays in the air, I have more time off and better pay. By the time I get home from AquaCool, there's very little day left. One evening I leave directly for the farm in Maryland to ride my horse. I am stuck in rush hour traffic on Route 1, then on the Wilson Bridge and the Beltway. Nearly two hours later I arrive at the farm. I have only an hour to saddle Sizzler and ride before it will be dark outside.

Another night I decide to get my hair cut. It's grown much longer than I ever wear it, shaggy and annoying. I haven't had a hair cut since the day I had my hair follicle sample taken and Zefan tried to repair it. I worry that I might need another sample for testing and I don't want to destroy any evidence. Roger finally agrees a haircut is okay.

The shop is busy. Several people are ahead of me. All these people work days, like me now, and try to cram all other activities into their evening hours. Zefan has gone home. She only works days too. I hate not having any days off during the week.

I don't know when I'll be able to come back during the day. Another stylist cuts my hair. Usually I wear it very short, close to a buzz. This stylist tries but thinks she is cutting way too much. I encourage her to cut more. It's not enough but it will have to do for now.

I go home. I want my so-called normal life back.

Friday, August 6, 1999

AFTER A HARD day at the office, we're home trying to have a "normal" dinner. Roger tells me USAirways announced plans to offer travel, medical and pension benefits to domestic partners of nonmarried employees, like us. We have an ongoing good-natured competition about our respective employers. This evens the playing field.

A day earlier, American Airlines made a similar announcement and last week United Airlines announced domestic partner benefits. The announcement means travel benefits similar to spouse privileges. Details are not available but we will need to submit a notarized affidavit of a domestic relationship, plus proof of joint residence and financial interdependence.

"Now I don't need to get my airline job back because I can get travel benefits though you," I joke to Roger.

But he wants his benefits at American, too, so I'm not easily off the hook.

In any case, our new travel benefits would be an asset should we move and need to travel to another city to get to a crew base for work. It's an interesting and unexpected development.

We have lived together 10 years and have a home mortgage together. Meeting the criteria will be no problem.

"There tends to be a domino effect in some industries and that's what's happening in the airline industry right now," one official was quoted in a newspaper report.

16

"Opportunity dances with those already on the dance floor."

–M. Jackson Brown, Jr., *A Hero in Every Heart*

Saturday, August 7, 1999

EVERY SATURDAY MORNING, I curse under my breath as I drive the Beltway to Silver Spring. The class is educational but it goes beyond what was appropriate for my case. I consider it harsh. I've heard of another flight attendant going to three hours of films on alcohol to meet the education criteria for reinstatement after a positive drug test. And I'm attending eight weeks of class.

This week's subject is an overview of drug use, abuse and dependence. Nicotine is the nation's number one drug of abuse, followed by alcohol and marijuana. Addiction is a disease. Strong people have addictions, too. An addict is not necessarily weak. Nicotine is a stimulant; alcohol is a sedative.

The steps of addiction: Compulsive use, loss of control, continual use in spite of adverse consequences and denial. I'm learning stuff I don't need but it's not useless information either.

Sunday, August 8, 1999

I sleep in until nearly 10 am. The telephone is silent for a change. No flight attendants calling Roger with their crises. We decide to stay home and relax since there is a high probability of rain showers. Anyway, we can't ride the horses in this sweltering heat. Tomorrow we go back to New York. Today will be free of working on my drug case. Wrong plan.

The phone rings. It's our friend Sharon in Miami. She hopes we might have good news for her. She's disappointed.

"I wanted to ask if you heard about the Cuban guy who tested for cocaine this week and lost his medal," she says. "I read in the *Miami Herald* that they attributed it to something like drinking 10 cups of coffee. I thought it sounded like you, drinking all that coffee you do."

She hasn't saved the newspaper article and doesn't know the athlete's name. She thinks it was only two or three days earlier and she knows it was the Pan Am games. She gives us enough to search the Internet. Roger begins typing and eventually NewsLibrary Search yields the *Miami Herald* story from August 5: "Gold Winner in High Jump Was Positive for Cocaine."

The newspaper reports the Cuban high jump great and national celebrity Javier Sotomayor tested positive to 200 ng/ml of cocaine. Initially, it was explained that Sotomayor drank tea that might have contained cocoa leaves to cure an upset stomach. The theory was discounted, when a sample of the tea was analyzed and proven to be impossible to leave traces of cocaine in the urine.

Cuban officials, however, maintain Sotomayor's innocence and charge that he was the victim of sabotage. He has spoken out against recreational and performance-enhancing drug abuse. "His dignity is much above and beyond any results given in any laboratory," one official is quoted as saying.

A false lead, but we can't afford to ignore even the smallest clue. In any case, we empathize with Sotomayor's problem. The story of injustice sounds so familiar. Roger thinks we should contact Dateline, 20-20 and 60 Minutes to urge them to do a story on drug testing in the workplace.

"His story is parallel to yours," Roger says. "Only he is a celebrity."

As our DeskJet printer spits out the news stories, the phone rings again. It's a real estate agent who wants to show our house in 30 minutes. We haven't showered or dressed yet today. Papers are scattered everywhere. There are dishes in the kitchen sink. The kitty litter box needs to be cleaned. I have laundry strewn around the downstairs television room. We're both impatient and our nerves are on end.

"The hell with it," says Roger who doesn't feel like vacuuming and picking up. "They can see the house a mess. I don't care if we sell it or not anyway."

An hour later, a quiet and polite Korean family arrives, removes their shoes and walks through the house. We're not sure who the sales agent is and who the buyers are. We're having a difficult time communicating and we don't sense that they especially like or dislike the house. They jump when two cats jump out of a closet at them. We've been through this routine so many times. We don't give the showing another thought.

That night Roger and I venture into the city from our suburban refuge, the first time for me since I lost my job. Roger wants to treat me to dinner out. We feel like detectives returning to the scene of the crime, though we knew of no crime committed. We go back to Mr. Henry's for dinner, sitting on the patio but without rain tonight. Then we go to the country western nightclub where we had socialized the weekend before my random drug test.

The owner, Steve Smith, is a friend. He offers us cocktails and gives us a private tour of the upstairs where he's remodeling with an expansive oak bar. The mirrors and the impressive craftsmanship of the bar itself will make the room an appealing area. He's thinking about a drug testing program for his employees and wonders what I think.

"You think you could write a drug testing program?" Steve asks.

"I could write a book," I tell him. "I know enough about drug testing to put together a policy for you."

WE WATCH the show on the dance floor downstairs and chat with a friend visiting from out of town. By 10 pm, I'm ready to go home. I feel tired and old these days. A night owl most of my life, now I like to be in bed by midnight. I can't seem to get enough sleep.

We have a message waiting when we walk in the door. It's Mary Wharton, our real estate agent. She received an offer on our house this evening and needs to talk to us PDQ, as she likes to say. She wants to present the buyer's contract. It's too late to call her at home. Roger calls her office and leaves a voice mail message.

"Mary," he says. "We're going to New York tomorrow for the day. We're catching the 9 am USAirways Shuttle but we should be back by 3:30 or

4. We can meet with you then. Call us early or we'll try to reach you on our cell phone from New York."

17

"Usefulness is not impaired by imperfection. You can drink from a chipped cup."

–Greta K. Nagel

Monday, August 9, 1999

ROGER tries to reach Mary again before we leave for the airport but has no luck. He briefly considers staying home to review the offer on our house. He can't make the final decision without me so decides to make it wait until evening. I've gladly taken the day off from my temp job.

I can't go to the ticket counter and buy an employee pass to LaGuardia like I did a few weeks ago. So I call Roger's younger sister, Lou, to get a "companion ticket" since she's an airline employee, too.

I've known Lou–her real name is Roselle–as long as I've known Roger. I've helped her out before she had her travel benefits. Now she's helping me out.

A year ago in July, Lou came to Virginia to live with Roger and me. We were in Minnesota, where Lou lived at the time, with our horses and trailer for a rodeo. Lou had quit her job, ended a relationship and was suffering from alcohol and drug abuse problems. Her life was in upheaval.

Months before the rodeo, Lou had overdosed on pills and was drinking. She was depressed and had called Roger on her cell phone. With him in Virginia and another sister in Minnesota on the phone, they coaxed Lou through her crisis. Roger tricked Lou into driving to the house where she was staying and calling from a regular phone so he could identify her location if he needed to call the police. Then, they talked Lou into eating a raw egg and drinking dish soap to make her vomit. She was still troubled and unemployed when we rolled into town for the rodeo.

We offered her a free trip back to Virginia to live with us. She packed her clothes in some garbage bags and tossed them in our trailer the night before we left. In the morning, she was ready to leave and start a new life.

She knew Roger and I don't allow drugs in our home and that we rarely consume alcohol. An unopened beer will sit in our refrigerator for months. We've moved the same liquor bottles from house to house. Lou knew our home would be a safe and protected environment until she regrouped her life, got a job and her own place to live.

She learned about horses from us and traveled to other rodeos. The months weren't always easy. Lou worked only part-time and was short on money. She and Roger had conflicting opinions and personalities and I tried to not get between them. They argued about what she was and wasn't doing with her life.

Lou wanted to get an airline job and knew she couldn't until she finished her education. She was studying to get her GED since she hadn't graduated from high school. In November, she moved to Philadelphia, where she got her GED and was hired to work on the ramp for USAirways.

She's been clean of drugs for more than a year now. Her life has new direction and security. I'm proud to have been a positive influence and a part of the support team that helped her. Today, she did me a favor.

New York City

WE WALK through LaGuardia Airport, early for our appointment. Roger reaches Mary on the cell phone, setting an appointment for later in the afternoon. We go outside to smoke and Roger tries to get through on the phone to his crew scheduling to take a trip for tomorrow. He needs to get in his hours. He feels financial pressure building in our household. As a union rep, he has an "open schedule" and flies his trips around his "office" needs. I stop in the food court and buy Pepsis for us.

I feel like we keep going over and over the same ground. Still, I'm optimistic. We might have our house sold. And this trip brings me one step closer to going back to flying. We wait for Elyse's assistant to escort us through the secured area. We don't know the code on the door and I don't have a company ID badge.

Today we have pictures of our horses and Elyse seems fascinated by our cowboy lifestyle. She wants to know when we have a rodeo coming up that she could watch. She's back from a week's vacation and looks tanned. If it weren't for my appointment and another, she might not have come into work today, she says.

It's time to get down to business. I tell Elyse about the first four weeks of my drug education class. I assure her it's been a learning experience that I will take the knowledge with me for a long time.

Elyse's eyes bore into me and she lowers her voice. "You do understand you have to finish the class, even if you go back to work first," she says. I nod in agreement.

Elyse pulls out her follow-up evaluation paperwork and begins a series of questions.

"Can you assure me that you can return to work and stay drug and alcohol free?" she asks.

"Not a problem," I reply easily. She hands me a wallet-sized green laminated card. I know the card is the key to my reinstatement. I have no fear of drug testing itself but I am nervous about another error. I dread the impact daily testing will have on my day-to-day activities, mostly the inconvenience.

The card is for the Interactive Voice Response System. It reads, "This Call Will Help You Not To Use Today!" *As if using any drug was ever a problem, I think indignantly.*

I need to call this 800 number every day Monday through Friday on days when I'm not working, with the exceptions of days I might be traveling on vacation. When I call, I'll be told if I need to have a drug test on that day. If the voice response system says yes, I'll have to go to a collection site for a sample. Then I have to call back and report the specimen identification number that is being sent to the lab. The program is set up to last 24 months for an employee returning to work after a positive drug test.

"It's very important that you call in every day when you're not working and be tested if directed,"

Elyse says. "My office monitors the program although the rules are set up by DOT."

I need to furnish her with my monthly flying schedule so the days I don't call can be matched to the days I'm working. I can also call to be tested if I'm on a long layover in a city where AA Medical has offices. The more I call to be tested and get tested, the better the program works for me, she says.

When I'm home, I'll go to a lab in Sterling, VA, since we don't have AA Medical facilities in Washington. I recognize the name. It's the same contract facility that does the specimen collections at the Washington airports when an employee's number comes up for a random test. I already have the address and phone number in my DOT information file. I know the area. It's near Sandy and Jerry's house. Going there is a half-day's excursion.

"It's 45 miles away from our house," I tell Elyse. "Can I get a lab closer to my house?" She can set up the billing at another lab, provided it will do DOT-regulated chain of custody paperwork, if I provide her with the phone number. I'll call her tomorrow with the phone numbers of two labs.

Elyse checks her watch. She wants to get me over to AA Medical for a return-to-work drug test. If we hurry, we might catch the nurse before she closes for lunch hour. But the office is closed so we decide to catch some lunch and meet back with Elyse at 12:45.

AT 1 PM, the nurse is carefully going over the paperwork. She watches that I observe her open the box and follow each step of the procedure in order. I fill in and sign in all the necessary blanks. She hands me the cup and directs me to the bathroom, noting how much she will need for the split sample. *Like a split sample has ever helped anyone*, I think to myself.

I can't go but a little trickle of a stream. It's maybe a fourth of what the nurse told me she needs. I try harder and wait. I've never had this problem before. I've heard horror stories of flight attendants who couldn't urinate and waited hours. My bladder has always been cooperative. I've never been pee shy.

Today my nerves are working overtime. I wonder if I could have another false positive test for cocaine. I wait another 10 minutes in the stall, but there is nothing. I fear that if I don't come out of the bathroom soon, my sample will look suspicious. How long do I stay in here to keep trying?

Finally, I come out with the inadequate sample. The nurse is upset.

"This isn't enough," she says, "You have to do it over." She shakes her head. "Women have this problem, but rarely men."

"Now you'll need to wait an hour now before we can do it again," she says.

She looks in a refrigerator for a bottle of water but there is none. She directs me to the water fountain in the hall and says I'll have to wait until after 2 to retry.

In the waiting area, I tell Roger it will be another hour before I can leave. He jumps up, disbelief all over his face. He looks like he could strangle me. He's anxious to catch the 2 o'clock Shuttle back to Washington. We're scheduled to meet Mary at 4.

"You go on, I'll catch the 3 o'clock and meet up with you at Mary's office. I'll take the Metro from the airport to the King Street station," I say to Roger. "Her office has to be near there."

Roger leaves and I stay behind, getting up to drink from the water fountain every five minutes. In an hour, I drink what seems like a five-gallon bottle of Aqua Cool but it really was just airport tap water. I feel bloated but ready.

The second run is not dry and I have more than enough for the required sample. I'm out of there quickly.

I head for the Shuttle gate with plenty of time and seats on the flight. I stop at the men's room on the concourse. Once the flight takes off, I crawl over the man in the aisle seat to go again. I have to pee again as soon as we land in Washington and first thing when I get to Mary's office. It's Niagara Falls and it doesn't stop for the rest of the day.

It's 4:15 when I walk into Mary's office. Roger is sitting in the waiting area. Mary is behind schedule and on her way. The receptionist offers me something to drink. I shake my head no and grin. I don't think so, but thanks anyway.

The offer on our house is low. We debate a counter offer and check on some comparative sales in the neighborhood. We want to sell but can't afford to take a loss. We have to walk away from closing with cash to put down on another property, whether it's in Maryland near the horses or in Tennessee. Mary works the numbers until we are satisfied. It's a go.

The next day, our counter offer is countered. Our patience is being tested. Roger says this is our last and best offer. We come back one last time.

18

"Sometimes you're the windshield, sometimes you're the bug..."

–Singer Mary Chapin Carpenter

Alexandria, VA
Wednesday, August 11, 1999

THREE DAYS after the opening offer, Roger calls me at Aqua Cool. He's headed to the airport and will be gone for three days. The house deal is accepted and Mary is leaving the final papers at our house. Closing is 45 days away, Sept. 27. We're moving. We just don't know where.

"We've got to go to Tennessee," he says urgently. "We've got to do something. Talk to you later."

And I need to get my reinstatement resolved. But I'm at this job where I don't have a minute to make a personal phone call to resolve unfinished business in my life. Roger is still working at home on researching my drug testing case but my activities have come to a nearly a dead halt. We haven't received the litigation package for the split sample and we haven't received the seals from either sample.

In the evening, I'm playing telephone tag with Laura and Elyse about my reinstatement. I leave messages for Laura who is setting up a meeting with Human Resources to get the paperwork done.

"I was trying for Washington but it fell through," she says on my voice mail, which I retrieve when I get home that evening. "We can do it in Dallas on Thursday or Friday. I can't be there Friday but I can get someone in Dallas to be there with you. Or you can wait until Monday or Tuesday in Washington. Let me know."

By the time I get the message, it's too late in the day to set up travel arrangements and get the right people together for a meeting on Thursday. But I'll go Friday. I want to do this as soon as possible. I want to be flying next week. Roger has talked to Laura. I'd like him to go with me but it would be on his own.

Meanwhile, Elyse has called. The first lab I referred her to doesn't do DOT chain of custody testing. She called the other lab but has not been able to get to the right person to set up the necessary billing. I sense something amiss but I can't put my finger on it.

"I don't have time to go and call labs," her voice mail message to me says. "You need to do that. AA will provide the lab with the kits. They need to do the collection process and paperwork and it gets sent to our lab. I usually work out the fee for the collection. I'll work out the payment setup if you get the contact person."

The ball is back in my court. I manage to call the SmithKline office on Duke Street and tell the lab technician my story. She gives me an 800 number to call to reach her supervisor. I reach the supervisor and tell my story another time. Yes, they can do DOT chain of custody collection. She gives me another number to call to set up the billing arrangements. I call Elyse and give her another number for SmithKline.

I call Express Personnel on Thursday to tell them I won't be coming back to this assignment. I tell Rita it's my last day at Aqua Cool. She's sad. She wants me to call her if I have extra days I can come in to work for her.

"You're like having two people quit on me at the same time," she says. "I'll miss you. You caught on quickly and worked hard."

The rest of the staff is excited for me, asking if I can get them some free tickets when I go back to my airline job. They want to know if I ever go to any exciting places. Yeah, I laugh, El Paso and Detroit. They think the job must be glamorous. I know I like it better than being chained to a telephone and computer 8-to-5, five days a week. The phones have stopped ringing. Rita thinks it's odd that none of us are on the phone. She checks the monitor to see if we all have our lines blocked. No. Customers must be getting their water today.

19

"Any fact facing us is not as important as our attitude towards it, for that determines our success or failure."

–Norman Vincent Peale

Friday, August 13, 1999

IF I WERE superstitious, I wouldn't have picked this date for this important meeting.

I'm stopped at the security entrance to the American Airlines concourse at National Airport. The guard wipes the handles of my briefcase. I've never seen this before. *Do I look suspicious today? Is he checking for drugs or what?* He says the test will be over in a few seconds. He sticks the wipe cloth under a machine. He tells me he's checking for residue of explosives.

There is confusion at the departure gate. Passengers are leaving to go to another gate, and then they're back. I have to check in with my driver's license since I don't have a company ID. I'm traveling on company business.

A coworker is in line with her daughter who's traveling on the same flight. She asks me what I'm doing. Obviously, I'm not working. Flight attendants are a curious group, always inquiring about each other when we travel. Usually we run into each other on airplanes and in airports while heading to exotic vacation destinations. Not me.

Out of earshot of passengers I tell her discreetly. It's impossible to not talk about my activities of the past two months.

It's not unusual to go months, even a year and not see a coworker if you don't socialize outside of work. We work odd schedules at different airports. We spend a few intense days together on a trip and then we're back in our own worlds.

When someone has a baby, it's posted on the bulletin board at the crew base with a cute picture. When a crewmember loses a parent or family member, it's posted on the system e-mail for flight attendants to read. When you're fired for a positive drug test, you're expected to go away quietly.

My colleague is amazed, as is everyone.

"You?" she asks incredulously. "You?"

Two hours later at the DFW Airport, I'm looking for Greg Hildreth, the APFA rep who will attend my reinstatement meeting with me. A good-looking model-type, Laura told Roger when she was making my travel arrangements. I approach a man waiting for someone. No, he says. I look up and Greg waves at me from across the hall.

We shake hands and he asks if I want coffee. No, I say, but can we talk? We head to a nearby food court. I have broader issues than just getting my job back, I tell him.

"I'm frustrated with the lack of enthusiasm by the union," I tell Greg, my voice quivering. "I'm frustrated by a union that represents flight attendants who don't perhaps deserve getting their jobs back, who abuse their sick time and other job benefits. For my entire career, I've given to the company and to the union. No one seems willing to stick his or her neck out for me. I've been told the APFA lawyer would call me. In seven weeks I've heard nothing.

I ask Greg how much he knows about cocaine. I tell him how easily cocaine can be absorbed into your system, through your hands, and how low my confirmation tests were.

"Does the union have any data on test results of flight attendants who have tested positive for cocaine?" I ask. "How would my results compare to someone who has admitted using the drug? I believe there would be a difference."

Greg shakes his head. He seems to realize I'm venting frustrations as much as anything. He doesn't take my ranting personally. His pager goes off. It's time for us to go. He leads me outside security to find the conference room for our meeting. Larry Sharp from Human Resources is already in the room. We take seats opposite him at the table. My most recent urinalysis must be back with a negative result or we wouldn't be here.

I tell Larry my concerns are broader than just getting my job back, that I want to continue to work cooperatively in addressing concerns about drug testing in our workplace. I'd like an addendum on my reinstatement to state such intentions.

"I believe the implications in my case go beyond me and should be the concern of the company," I say. "I would like to have a cooperative relationship. I want to state on the record of my hope to work with AA Medical or other appropriate persons."

Larry seems to follow me but there is no place at this meeting to make such a plan. We proceed to the reinstatement. I must sign three copies of the papers. Also, I must sign an undated letter of resignation which will be effective immediately should I have another positive drug test.

I accidentally date one of the resignation letters with today's date. Greg takes it and rips it up and throws the scraps in his bag. Larry goes to get another copy of it.

I have seven days to sign the agreement. I see no purpose in waiting. I need to go back to work and seven more days isn't likely to uncover the mystery of my test.

The standard agreement acknowledges my educational program approved by EAP and the Return-to-Duty drug test but it neither admits nor denies any illicit drug usage. The agreement also states:

"You will withdraw all your grievances, protests, or appeals and waive and release all other claims, if any, against the Company, relating to your termination. Your acceptance of the terms and conditions of this agreement shall constitute such withdrawal, waiver, and release as well as acknowledgment that this agreement constitutes a complete, final, and binding settlement of all matters relating to your termination."

It goes on to say I will comply with the monitoring program of EAP for two years, submit to follow-up urinalysis and maintain complete abstinence from drugs, except with medical authorization.

I won't lose any seniority and the termination will be changed to administrative leave on my employment record. I won't get back pay or anything for all the overtime I missed out on this summer. Of course, all the out-of-pocket expenses incurred are mine alone. But I don't lose my accrued sick time.

It's a thin line I'm walking. I want the job back. I haven't signed a confession to something I didn't do. But I have signed away my fight against the company. In many ways, I'm disappointed. I've chosen survival. I need to move on with my life. Still, there is something I can do. I want to educate other flight attendants about drug testing. I don't want others in my situation to be left with so few resources, so little information.

I sign the papers. It's over in 30 minutes. I'm listed on a later flight back to Washington but Larry tells me two are leaving sooner, one in 10 minutes, another in 25 minutes. If I get to the gate, they'll bump me up.

I tell Greg I need to go outside to smoke before I board my airplane. He's surprised I smoke and he joins me.

"Do you think I'm nuts?" I query him. "Do I make any sense at all to you?"

He tells me that the APFA could use a drug testing coordinator and he is going to pass on the idea. My experience and knowledge would lend itself to such a position, if created by the board of directors, he says. Of course creating and filling such a position would be a political decision and I shouldn't hold out hopes.

We promise to keep in touch and I run for my gate. For the first time in months, my heart is pumping with excitement. The good kind.

From the airplane phone, I call home.

"I signed it," I tell Roger. "Would you call Scott and let him know I'm on my way? I should land at about 4:30. See if he'll stay so I can get my ID back. If he's not in, talk to Joy Simmons, the base manager." I give him telephone numbers and hang up.

OPERATIONS back in Washington is quiet. Scott, my supervisor, is not here. But Joy is behind her desk, working on her computer. It's the first time I've seen her since I was removed from my trip back in June. She greets me and tells me she talked to Roger. I imagine he entertained and charmed her, as he does.

She's reading an e-mail message from Larry Sharp. Apparently there is a complication with the paperwork since I left Dallas. Some piece of the paperwork hasn't moved from one office to the next office. Joy refuses to give me my crew ID. I don't understand what the holdup is.

"I'll call you on Monday," she promises. "If you don't hear from me, you call."

I had hoped to be flying by Monday. Yeah, right. It took a month to be terminated. Any expectations that getting back to work would move more quickly are dreams in my head.

AT HOME, two interesting pieces of mail are waiting on the kitchen table. First, I open the letter from the Virginia Employment Commission. I fear another disappointment and I want to get it over with first.

I am so wrong. The Deputy Commissioner believes there is reasonable doubt in my case and has ruled in my favor to qualify for benefits. The notification outlines my discharge, my statement that I never used cocaine, and that I had a hair follicle test done which was found negative.

"You did not cut your hair between the time the first test was done through your employer until the hair follicle test," states the ruling. "The Virginia Unemployment Compensation Act provides that an individual shall be disqualified if it is found that he was discharged as a results of misconduct in connection with work. Misconduct exists when it is shown that there was a willful, or substantial disregard of the employer's interest or standards of behavior that the employer has the right to expect of his employee.

"In view of the above, it is the opinion of the Deputy that there is insufficient evidence to show your actions constituted misconduct within the meaning of the act. You are, therefore, entitled to receive benefits."

I feel somewhat vindicated by the agency I had least expected to favor me. It's a minimal financial boost but a major psychological boost. I've been told unemployment benefits usually favor the employer, not the employee. Still, I feel the ruling is a small victory in a long battle.

Then I open a blue envelope, a Shoebox Greetings card, from Michelle Bertapelle. A check falls on floor. I pick it up. It's $200 made out to me.

On the front of the card is a bear stretched out, clinging to two trees: "Some days it's tougher to hang in there than others."

Michelle writes: "I can't wait to fly with you again. One of the things that have really bothered me about this whole process is your forced isolation from your coworkers. I mean, if someone becomes ill and can't work 'Wings' is there to help them out. But in your case, the system failed you. So last month I picked up a 2-day trip for you. It was really easy and my crew was so much fun. I didn't even feel like I was working…"

I'm choked up. I can't keep this money.

"Well, you can't insult her by sending it back either," Roger retorts.

20

"You can tell a lot about a town from how it treats its visitors."

–Mary E. Potter in *Berkshire Eagle*

Saturday, August 14, 1999

ALCOHOL and driving is this week's class topic. I never knew the difference between a DUI (Driving Under the Influence) and a DWI (Driving While Intoxicated). Now I know. We also discuss blood alcohol levels and the effects on the body at different levels and the speed at which the body metabolizes and gets rid of alcohol.

Alcohol is not a stimulant but a depressant, says Lynn, the facilitator, and it affects almost every part of the body. It leaves fat deposits in the liver from filtering the impurities. It affects the pancreas and kidneys, depletes the body of calcium for your bones and inhibits white blood cell production in your blood.

Oxygen is required to "detoxify" alcohol so it takes oxygen from brain cells, causing damage there as well.

After an hour and a half, my reservations about alcohol use and abuse are strongly reinforced.

I stop to call Roger at the front desk before he leaves for work.

"Should I get you a ticket on USAirways to go to Nashville?" he asks. "I called the listing agent for the house/barn. Do you want to go on Monday? We need to look at property."

"Sure," I say without enthusiasm, torn between my immediate hope of returning to active duty as a flight attendant next week and the need to resolve our living/moving situation.

Sunday, August 15, 1999

BY MID-AFTERNOON, the real estate agent in Tennessee calls back to confirm plans for tomorrow. She's on her cell phone and her voice cuts in and out as she drives over some Tennessee hills. Cell phones are a great technological advance that keep the world in touch. But when they don't work well, they are so aggravating. The agent is in the middle of another big property sale and is rushing to keep up with the involved parties.

"Roger and I are flying in Monday," I tell her. "We'll be traveling standby so you never know what will happen. If we get on the nonstop flight, we'll be in Nashville by 10:30 in the morning."

"Shall I pick you up?"

"No. That's not necessary. I know you're busy. We'll rent a car and meet you at your office by about 11:30."

She says she may not be available but another agent in the office is her backup and will help us. They will do a listings search and have some properties ready for us to consider.

"What are you looking for?" she asks.

"Property with a barn suitable for the horses is my first concern," I say. "The house is a lower priority for me. Roger has always wanted a log home. We do have some differing views. A reasonable drive from the Nashville airport and the price are major considerations for both of us."

"We can find something that suits all your needs," she says confidently.

Monday, August 16, 1999

THE ALARM goes off at 7 am and we're showered and dressed to go with a cup of coffee under our belts by 8. Do we pack an overnight bag? I want to go and get back the same day. I'm hoping to be put on a work schedule soon and don't want to miss it.

"This isn't something we're going to get done in one day," Roger tells me. "You're not going to work this week anyway," he predicts.

I stare out the window as Roger drives us to the airport. I can't bear to look at him. He's excited and anxious. How he can be so full of hope? Where does he get the energy to maintain through all this? He's irritated by my distraction. We each have a different focus this morning and we drive to the airport in silence.

The USAirways flight is full and our chances of getting on to Nashville are slim. We check in and wait for our names to be called. The door closes and the flight is gone–without us.

We head for the gate for a departing Pittsburgh flight. If we get to Pittsburgh, we can connect to Nashville and be there at 3:30. We recheck the timetable and wait. That flight boards and leaves as well–without us.

Do we go home and come back for the next nonstop flight at 5 pm? No, we'll try making the Philadelphia flight that would connect us into Nashville at 4 pm. We check in wait and they call our names. We board a shuttle bus to go out to the commuter plane. Roger calls his sister Lou in Philly and tells her to meet us.

"We're coming through," he says. "We'll do lunch at the airport. We have two hours before we depart for Nashville."

I have the flight timetable in my hand. I give Roger the phone number of the real estate office in Lebanon. He calls and leaves a message that we missed our first flight and we're going around Robin

Hood's barn to get there. We'll call when we arrive later in the afternoon.

The flight is turbulent and the flight attendant is way too cheerful, sing songing the announcements, putting emphasis on all the wrong places. She sounds like she's singing a preschool nursery rhyme. We try to read our paperbacks but it's impossible with all that going on.

Lou and police officer friend Jennifer meet us as we pass through security at the Philadelphia airport. It's the first time I've seen Lou in her work uniform. She looks good, quite a dramatic change from the bedraggled sibling we brought to Virginia just over a year ago with her clothes thrown in garbage bags. We go outside to smoke and then decide to find a place for lunch. We sit at Fridays and eat a long lunch. We have two hours before our Nashville departure.

Time to boogie. We find the gate and get in line to check in. Roger asks me for the tickets. I think he has them. He checks his briefcase. Not there. We get out of line and dig through my overnight bag. Not there.

Roger goes through the briefcase again. Not there. We have 25 minutes before departure.

I'm stuck in the proverbial canoe without a paddle. I don't remember seeing the tickets since we left Washington. I don't have airline employee travel benefits. I can't get tickets for myself like I'm accustomed. Roger has used his yearly allotment of companion tickets, my trip to Nashville being his last. There isn't an immediate way to replace lost tickets at the gate. His patience is tissue paper thin.

Lou. I ask Lou if I can use another of her newly acquired companion tickets. Okay. We run, me pulling her with her short legs, down the concourse. The clock is ticking. There isn't a long line but each passenger ahead of us seems to take an eternity. 10 minutes until departure.

The agent doesn't understand that I lost half of my tickets to Nashville, having originated in Washington. She can't seem to reissue the remaining legs of the trip so I finally tell her to write a round-trip from Philly. If I can't get the return trip changed, Lou will drive me home from Philly.

I sprint, clutching the tickets in my hand. Of course, our gate is the last on the concourse. It's departure time. I see no one left at the gate. Roger is walking away from the counter. He sees me, grabs the tickets and opens the jet bridge door. We run. The agents have been trying to help Roger but there's nothing they can do. They have stalled just a few moments in case I make the run.

"Take any open seat," an agent says as she closes the door.

I settle a row behind Roger, catching my breath. He glares at me with an evil eye. I nearly caused us to miss the flight. I can almost see the steam coming out of his ears. We don't talk until the plane touches down in Nashville.

"I'll call the real estate office and let them know we're here," I say. "I'll go pick up the rental car."

He turns toward the USAirways ticket counter to straighten out my lost ticket/wrong new ticket problem.

"I'm moving here to become a country western star," I hear him tell the agent as he tries to warm her up to our ticket problem. The agent gives Roger a lost-ticket form to fill out and submit for a refund.

As we head east out of Nashville in the rental car, the rocky bluffs along Interstate-40 seem unfamiliar to Roger. I tell him we've been down this road many times. The scenery looks different from a small rental car than from our truck and horse trailer rig.

For the moment, I'm enjoying the adventure. My drug test and temporary unemployment are pushed to the back of my mind.

Lebanon, Tenn.

This city, named for the Biblical Lands of Cedar, is a rural town with a population of 19,000, busting out at its seams with its convenient location to Nashville 20 miles away. Development is booming and the city limits have been expanded and area land annexed. Its diplomat-free culture is a world, not two states, away from Washington, DC. This is Middle America, not unlike the rural Minnesota community where I grew up.

It has its own daily newspaper, 34 churches, a large hospital, three high schools, and Cumberland University. There's talk of the 1,600-acre Nashville Superspeedway being built south of town.

Lebanon is the Wilson County seat and home to Cracker Barrel headquarters with some 700 employees. Jobs seem to be plentiful with Hartman Luggage, TRW, Toshiba American, Wynn's Precision, Fortune Plastics and Pillow-Teck all having manufacturing plants here. Many craftsmen have their own businesses and there is a flea market at every intersection.

The climate is mild. Average annual temperature is 62 and the average temperature in January is 40. The county's median household income in 1998 was $43,932, second highest ranking in the state of Tennessee.

Like many Tennessee towns, Lebanon has a town square, graced by a statute of Brigadier Gen. Robert Hopkins Hatton, honoring the 1,000 or more Confederate volunteers from Wilson County. This is the South! It's not unusual to see a Confederate flag flying in someone's yard. Hatton, who died in the Battle of Seven Pines defending Richmond, VA, had attended Cumberland University and served as a U.S. Congressman.

While most businesses have moved to the outskirts of downtown, the remaining tenants on the square mostly are antique shops, with the exception of a Burger King and a travel office.

Cumberland Real Estate office is located on west side of the square. The real estate office is a turn-of-the-century building renovated to keep its old charm. Heavy oak doors and 20-foot pressed-tin ceilings give it a solid, reliable feeling.

Susie Goodall greets us. She's dressed casually with lace up boots for walking farm property, an armful of papers, purse and "fixin" to tour us around the countryside. She may have grown up in Philadelphia but she has acquired a Tennessee twang that goes well with her coal-black hair.

She has done a property search and has about a dozen listings near or in our price range, including the house built inside the horse barn. We want to see it and put it out of our minds or decide to pursue it. Susie heads us out to the property. We will study the other listings this evening and start out in the morning.

We like the barn/house but we're not overwhelmed. The living space is…Mmm…interesting, sort of a rustic lodge. We would need to do considerable renovation to be happy with it. Before we return to Washington, we'll be back for a second time to reexamine the possibilities.

That night we check into the local Holiday Inn Express, have dinner at Applebee's and sort through the property listings from Susie. If the friendly waitress is any example of local hospitality, we would like it here.

Tuesday, August 17, 1999

IN THE MORNING, after filling up at the local Waffle House, we head out of town in our rental car to preview a property before meeting up with Susie. The property we want to see is a log home with a small barn on Simmons Bluff Road. We can't find the road and eventually turn back to town to meet up with Susie and begin our touring drive. We eliminate several properties without going into the houses. Three different properties with log homes look promising, but may be out of our price range. Still, we're hopeful.

As we drive, I wonder what to tell Susie about my drug-testing problem. There isn't an easy explanation so the issue remains undisclosed.

At noon, we pull into MacDonald's for a quick lunch. I go outside to a pay phone while Roger and Susie sit down to eat. I haven't received any telephone messages at home about returning to work. So much for hearing from Joy on Monday! I call flight service, get an answering machine and leave a message. I'll be back in Washington tonight and would like to get a work schedule this week.

At 6 pm, we're on board our fight home.

"ARE YOU READY to do this?" Roger asks as we drive down the George Washington Parkway toward home that evening. He waves toward the townhomes along the street. "Are you ready to leave this all behind?"

"Three months ago, I had doubts about leaving Washington. My attitude is so changed now. I would always think of this terrible summer as long as I live in our house here. The memories aren't good. Every day now I'm writing about my case and it's been good therapy. I didn't realize I missed my writing as much as I do."

We agree it's time to move on with our lives, drug test or not.

Thursday, August 19, 1999
Alexandria, Va.

IT'S BEEN TWO days since we were in Tennessee. One property with a log home stands out in our minds. We pull out the listing and stare at the picture. After seeing so many properties in just a few hours, I'm confused about which one is which.

This one is the 13 acres on top of a hill off Simmons Bluff Road that we couldn't find on our solo trek out of town. From the outside, the house is deceivingly small. But inside, it has two bathrooms and four bedrooms, a stone fireplace in the middle of the downstairs and front and back porches that overlook the property.

There is a view of the surrounding countryside for several miles. Trees along one side and large open fields would make a perfect home for us and the three-stall barn would suit our horses. A mile down the road is Cedars of Lebanon State Park, a great place for trail riding on the horses. It would be a fitting end to the current turmoil in our lives.

We call Susie to make an offer. Roger calls our mortgage company to get preapproval on a loan.

Meanwhile, I'm trying to get a schedule for work. I call Laura. I call Juan. I call the local flight service office. I call Larry Sharp at Human Resources to find out what the hold up is. As usual, I don't get real people and I leave messages.

Then I hear from Elyse at EAP. She has not been able to set up my testing program at the SmithKline lab in Alexandria because she hasn't reached the right person to set up the billing. I tell her to forget it. I'll just drive to Sterling, VA, to have my urinalysis when necessary. I can't afford to wait any longer to go back to work. I suspect the holdup in returning me to work is paperwork from Elyse over the follow-up testing.

The week is nearly over and I'm "on the payroll" but have no schedule and no computer access. Joy, the base manager, calls me at home Thursday evening. She assures me several staff members will be working on the problem in the morning. If I don't hear from them by noon, I should call and check in. Individually, no one is held responsible. Collectively, there is mass confusion. It is the American way. I'm told someone in Tulsa is waiting for drug test results. No one in Tulsa has anything to do with my drug test. I don't understand.

Joy mentions that crewmembers working my flight in from DFW last week inquired at the office about me. Flight service, like AA Medical, Human Resources and EAP, even my APFA representatives, all are bound to confidentiality and can't talk about my case. I can. I have nothing to hide. In fact, I believe flight attendants actually need more education about drug testing, chemical dependency, and how they may unknowingly expose themselves to drugs.

"We should probably keep this under our hats," she urges me.

"I see," I reply.

The only hat I ever wear is a cowboy hat and I wear that only at rodeos. I have nothing to hide and don't plan to keep the truth a secret.

The rumor mill must be working overtime. Like the saying goes, you should only worry when they *stop* talking about you. I'm sure speculation will be rampant when coworkers learn that I'm moving away at the same time this has happened.

Friday, August 20, 1999

THE DEADLINE for bidding for our flying schedules for September is a few hours away. If I don't bid, I risk not getting control of my work schedule for another month. All day long Friday I'm on the phone, inquiring about my work status. Finally, at 5 pm, I can access the computer, though it won't allow me to bid for next month. However, I'm told, tomorrow I should be able to schedule myself for a trip, leaving Sunday.

Oddly, the computer says I'm based in BUF, which is Buffalo, NY, an old crew base closed by American years ago. I'm told BUF is computer limbo where inactive flight attendants are placed. Inactive is not a word I want to use for myself.

At 7 pm, I've talked to Juan on her cell phone several times and finally concede a loss to the computer system. I'm over it. I won't stress out any longer. Juan says she can call Joy at home and try to resolve the problem.

"That's okay," I tell her. If I can't bid, the company will just have to build a September schedule honoring the days off I would have sought in bidding. Juan concurs.

Earlier Friday, we've received a counter proposal on the Tennessee property. It's not acceptable but we're moving in the right direction. Roger is on a trip and we talk that evening. We decide on a counter to the counter that I will give to Susie the next day.

AT 11 O'CLOCK that evening, I'm in the kitchen on the phone with a friend. She and her husband also are moving cross-country from St. Louis to Charlotte. There's plenty of drama in their lives, too. A loud pounding on my front door interrupts our conversation. *Urgent and odd for this hour of the night.* I tell my friend I'll call her back.

I rush to the door and pull it open. A Fairfax County police officer pulls out his badge.

"Is this your residence?" he asks.

I'm startled, bewildered. I nod my head yes. I'm not dressed for company. I'm wearing just boxer shorts.

"We just arrested a suspect in your backyard," the officer tells me. "He ran from the scene on Route 1 a block away and jumped over the fence into your yard. Three boards are broken. We arrested him in your yard."

"Okay-y-y."

"We may need you to testify if we charge him with trespassing on personal property. Can I get your name and phone number?"

I give him my name and Roger's and tell him we are moving next month. He asks me to keep in touch.

After he leaves, I return to the kitchen and turn on the back yard light. Sure enough. Three boards on the fence are knocked down. And to think I never heard the commotion!

It is a good time to move. Less than two years ago, the first month after moving in, the windshield on my truck was shot with a pellet gun by a 15-year-old neighbor boy. The youth finally admitted the vandalism when I called the police and an officer confronted the boy. After a couple of months he got a job and paid for the replacement windshield. It was an eye-opening experience for him and me.

Yes, it's good that we're leaving this house, this neighborhood, and this town.

Saturday, August 21, 1999

AT 6:30 AM, I'm up and working on the computer to find available trips I can work on Sunday. I try to put myself on a trip via the telephone access number. It doesn't accept my prompts. I call crew scheduling and explain to a live person what has happened. The scheduler asks what trip I want and she puts it through. Very simply.

Seven weeks of Saturday drug education class completed. One more to go. Will I be more knowledgeable for my $240 investment? Without a doubt.

Class this week focuses on cocaine, a subject I've been anxiously awaiting. Lynn explains how drug marketing brought about widespread use of crack cocaine. Cocaine in its powdered form is expensive. Traffickers figured out that if it was processed into smaller, salable units in the "rock" form for smoking it could be purchased at $10 a shot by the masses instead of the high prices afforded by the well to do.

"Think about it," Lynn explains. "You're hungry and you have a dollar in your pocket. A small can of tuna is $1 and that's all you can afford. Even if a larger can is more economical, you can't afford it."

Cocaine works by flooding the reward/pleasure center of your brain and releasing dopamine, the same chemical that gives you an orgasm high. It increases the levels of adrenaline, causes muscle tremors and releases serotonin, causing sensations of pleasure. These account for temporary feelings of contentment and animated confidence.

The high lasts for about 10 minutes, but its effects on the brain are long-term. The brain is depleted of its natural level of dopamine and then you start to rely on the drug for happiness. Long-term use can result in stimulant-induced psychosis, hyperactivity, paranoia, aggression, delusions, anxiety and insomnia.

After class, I head to the farm. I call Susie with our compromise proposal and saddle my horse for an afternoon ride. Around 3 pm, Susie calls. Our compromise offer was accepted. I literally jump up and down in the kitchen. I'm going to work tomorrow *and* we're getting the log home in Tennessee.

Denise glares at me. We're going to miss our best friends terribly.

"Tennessee is a long ways away," Dickie says later. "Can't you find a farm around here?"

A FEW DAYS later, I'm on the phone with one of my always-joking younger brothers back in Minnesota.

"Are you going to get two names, like Billy Bob, like they do in the South?" he asks me.

"I hear possum pie is really popular there, made from road kill," he chides me.

He would be amused to know there is a Possum (not Opossum) Town, a small Mayberry-like unincorporated community about four miles northwest of Lebanon.

21

"Freedom to be your best means nothing unless you're willing to do your best."

–Colin Powell

Sunday, August 22, 1999

I FEEL LIKE a new hire getting ready for work Sunday morning. I pull my Roller board from the closet. It is covered with cat hair. I wrap tape around my hand and attempt to clean it up. Packing for an overnight requires more thought than I remember. What do I bring for layover clothes? I put on my union pin, leaving my special "Info Rep" pin on the dresser. I don't feel like I can honestly represent my union anymore.

I cruise down the George Washington Parkway to National Airport. The sun seems brighter than I've seen all summer as it peeks through the clouds. Is this the end of my story? They have a urine specimen with a trace element of cocaine. The test doesn't tell when or how it got there. Even if it's truly mine, we may never know for sure. I have a mark against my name. It's hard for me to accept, but it's time to move on with life. I want to put aside my bitterness and anger. I want to get on with what I always felt was a good, satisfying life.

In the crew operations area, I sign in for my trip. I'm watching my back. I'm paranoid. I see a flashing neon sign in my head, *EXPECT THE UNEXPECTED. LOOK OUT.* I expect the phone to ring and someone to tell me I'm not going to be working today.

I enter a request in the computer system for a transfer to the New York crew base. I'm outa here. The next round of transfers will be posted late in September. I'm moving on.

I'm working on a Boeing 757, just like back in June when I drug tested and later learned of the drug test results. One of my crewmembers has been flying just eight weeks, less time than I've been away. Interestingly, I'm headed to Miami, my first flight back.

I greet passengers as they board and hang coats for first class passengers. It's good to be back. The captain turns on the seat belt sign and the agent closes the entry door. The safety video plays and we check to see that the passengers are all buckled in and have their carryons properly stowed.

I'm strapped in my jump seat, again just behind the first class section. The plane shakes and I feel the engines rumble and groan. After nine years of working on airplanes, takeoffs still give me a thrill. We roll down the runway and I feel us lift into the sky. The jet cuts through the clouds and we're now in a box of cotton, a white sterileness below and a seemingly endless infinity above us. Miami, here I come.

As I've gone back to work, I've also begun calling every day off for the required follow-up drug testing. The first two days I get a "No. No test required today" message.

The third day I get the message, "Yes, test today. Please call ahead to the testing site to check their hours." I call Parametrics to check their office hours and get directions.

I drive to Sterling, VA, and pee in the cup. I crawl with the stop-and-go Beltway traffic and get home 2 1/2 hours later. Then I call the 800 number again and report the specimen number. The program is an excellent system for assisting an addict to stay clean. It's a bit overboard for someone who's been twice evaluated as non-addicted. In fact, I'm outraged that I'll be doing this for two more years, not to mention the company resources that are being spent to pay for it and my own time on my days off it will consume.

In the first three months back at flying, my "number" will come up for "follow-up" drug testing about once per month. In later months, I'm told to test as often as five times in a month, once four times in an eight-day period. I try to remember to call first thing every morning and plan errands around a trip to town and the collection site when I'm required to test. Some days I'll have to make the trek even if I wasn't planning to leave my house all day.

THE WORK routine also is bumpy. The termination and reinstatement has had a domino effect, triggering various problems. There are computer glitches not ironed out. One day in Los Angeles I was assigned at LAX to deadhead, or ride as a passenger, to my next destination. The agent is attempting to check me in but the computer keeps telling him, "Invalid Travel Card for This Employee." He checks my ID and the crew list. My name is there so he overrides the system and issues me a boarding pass and seat assignment anyway.

The next day back in Washington it happens again. The agent insists she won't board me and I don't want to argue with her in front of passengers. I go downstairs to American crew operations and sit myself in the base manager's office.

I ask Joy to fix the problem. She tells me the agent can override it. I tell her who the agent is and Joy recognizes the name immediately. I ask her to call the agent for herself. She calls the agent at the gate and Joy's assistant writes a "to whom it may concern" letter for me to carry while I'm on duty in case there are further problems.

Joy tells me the reinstatement hasn't caught up with the termination in the company's computer system.

As I sit in a passenger seat, I read the mini-book "A Spirit of Greatness," which American Airlines has placed in the seat back pockets. The book is a tribute to the courage and compassion of the company's employees and tells of people helping one another, customers and fellow employees, going the extra mile to make the difference.

"I think the single most important factor that makes American Airlines a great company is its total commitment to the needs of its customers, regardless of their nature or magnitude," writes a captain in one excerpt.

I wonder to myself. *What part of the picture am I missing? Why do I feel so much bitterness toward a company that prides itself on compassion, caring about its customers and its fellow employees? What went wrong for me? Where was the compassion when I was trying to clear my name? Why do I feel like I have an inoperable exit with every move I make?*

22

"Never give in. Never. Never. Never. Never."

—Winston Churchill

Thursday, August 26, 1999

I'VE BEEN BACK at work just four days. A huge drug bust at American Airlines in Miami is the talk of the day among travelers and airline employees. I hear the shocking news for the first time from two Southwest Airlines pilots riding on a crew van in Los Angeles.

"58 Indicted in Airline Drug Case," screams the banner headline across the top of the *Fort Worth Star-Telegram*.

"Airport Smuggling Ring Busted," announces the *Miami Herald*. "58 Indicted in Widespread Gun-Drugs Case."

The Associated Press reports:

"Airline Workers Held in Drug Probe"

By Meg Richards

MIAMI (AP) - Dozens of American Airlines ramp workers and contract employees were arrested and charged Wednesday in a drug ring that investigators said smuggled cocaine and marijuana into the United States in food carts, garbage bags and carryon luggage.

The bust is believed to be the biggest set of drug arrests involving a U.S. airline.

The arrests resulted from two sting operations, one of which was prompted in part when a pilot complained last year that his coffee tasted weak. Investigators discovered 15 pounds of heroin in coffee packs aboard an American plane.

The drugs were put aboard American Airlines planes in Colombia and Central America, flown to Miami, and then went on to Philadelphia, Washington, New York, Baltimore and Cleveland, investigators said. The defendants also allegedly smuggled guns and explosives that undercover agents had given them.

At least 50 people were indicted on drug charges, including 30 American baggage handlers and ground crew workers at Miami International Airport, where

American is the largest carrier. It is also the biggest U.S. airline serving Latin America.

Separately, eight people, including seven American employees, were indicted in New York in a similar case.

Also, officials in Colombia identified American as the airline used by 10 Colombians charged over the weekend with smuggling more than a half-ton of heroin to Miami.

"Greed is the bottom line. They did it all for a price," said Ed Halley, a spokesman for the Bureau of Alcohol, Tobacco and Firearms.

In the Miami and New York cases, no one in management was arrested, and no American pilots or flight attendants were indicted.

American said it has cooperated with investigators and blamed the problem on a "small group of employees."

"This is a company with zero tolerance for illegal drugs," said Larry Wansley, American's managing director of corporate security.

The Star-Telegram reports that Operation Sky Chef and Operation Ramp Rats found drugs hidden in airplane wall panels, overhead compartments, kitchen areas, suitcases, backpacks, and wheel bays. An Associated Press photo shows custom agents in Miami displaying a catering food cart that contained 41 pounds of cocaine stashed on an airplane.

In other smuggling cases, about 64 pounds of cocaine were found in March 1996 stuffed in the cockpit ceiling of a Boeing 757 parked at DFW Airport for an overnight maintenance check. The jet had made stops in Costa Rica, Guatemala, Puerto Rico and several U.S. cities before the drugs were found.

In 1997, seven American Airlines mechanics in Miami were charged with smuggling millions of dollars worth of heroin and cocaine from Columbia. The drugs were found in fishnet-type material behind panels in the ceilings, lavatories, kitchens and cockpits of several American airplanes.

It has to be a public relations nightmare for American, right up there with major air disasters. It's even fodder for editorial cartoonists. Mike Luckovich in the *Atlanta Constitution* depicts a passenger on an American flight holding up a pillow to a flight attendant, saying, "Excuse me, all the powder's coming out of this pillow…" The pillow is labeled 1 KILO.

In the *Times Picayune*, Matt Handelsman depicts the Justice Department holding a press conference on the "Baggage Handlers Drug Bust." The speaker says, "This undercover operation would have ended sooner, but the evidence got rerouted to Toledo and ended up in Scranton…"

To me, it's not a laughing matter. It's far too real. Who makes the coffee the pilots drink? And who drinks more coffee on the airplane than me? Who serves the food out of the carts? How many of the three Boeing 757s I worked on June 15 and 16 had been in Central or South America? American Airlines purchased these lucrative Latin routes from Eastern Airlines in the early 1990s. Were smuggled drugs concealed in those airplanes or in my carts and not removed as intended? Did some cocaine spill onto something I ate, drank or handled?

While previously I had considered passive exposure to cocaine from passengers, now I have to wonder about my immediate working environment. Was there reckless endangerment of our workforce while the drugs were smuggled on board and crewmembers were never warned?

It's time to work the phone again. I call Laura and Juan. I call the Drug Enforcement Agency in Miami and I call AA Corporate Security in Dallas.

At the DEA, Brent Eaton refers me to Customs in Miami. He says the DEA largely was involved in the smuggling onboard by "passengers" and that Customs handled drugs that were stashed in the food carts and on the aircraft.

I finally reach Suzanne Clark at corporate security and tell her my concerns. She promises to check it out. A few days later, Suzanne has called Joy, my base manager, and told her that no cocaine was *found* on the airplanes I was working during the trip prior to my infamous drug test. Joy calls me to pass on the information.

I hadn't given Suzanne my trip schedule so I wonder how she could put together that answer so quickly. I also wonder why corporate security couldn't call me directly, why the information had to be passed through a third party. I share my concern with Laura who says she will double check with corporate security. Later, I fax Laura my activity record for the month of June so she'll know exactly what flights I was working.

A few days later, I hear from Laura. She's been digging for information but uncovers nothing particularly encouraging for my case. Drugs indeed were being smuggled onboard. In the case of the heroin in the coffee, the smugglers had disabled the coffee maker so stored coffee packs wouldn't be used onboard the airplane. But an ingenious flight attendant fixed the problem and brewed coffee anyway. In regard to the food carts pictured in the newspaper with cocaine, Laura was told, those pictures allegedly were from drug busts two years earlier. The caption under the photo, however, says "displayed yesterday."

She has finally received copies of my first specimen seal and is sending those to me. She also has received the company's litigation package for the split test and is forwarding that to me. SmithKline is holding the second seal and they won't release a copy of it. Laura tells me she will go personally to the lab to view it when in Dallas in several weeks.

When I get the first seal, I compare the initials to those I've put on house sale papers recently and liquor deposit forms at work. The slant seems off. Should I have a handwriting expert examine them?

While direct word to employees from the company about the drug smuggling has been nil, Don Carty, American Airlines chairman, addresses the issue to passengers in his monthly column in *American Way* magazine.

"From the outset, American was an active and involved participant in the investigation," he writes. "In the process, we devoted significant company resources providing information and assistance to law enforcement authorities. You wouldn't expect anything less from American."

Last year, according to Carty, the company's own drug interdiction efforts resulted in the seizure of more than 3,100 pounds of contraband from American Airlines aircraft, almost twice the amount that U.S. Customs inspectors found at the airports American serves.

"We want to personally assure you that our commitment to the safety and security of our passengers and employees is absolute," he continues.

Not four months later, American would plead guilty to the criminal conviction of mishandling hazardous cargo at the Miami airport and pay an $8 million fine, yet another public relations nightmare for the airline. Investigators would find what they called an alarming pattern that was not just a matter of negligence in handling shipments packed as cargo beneath planeloads of passengers.

Before a judge, Don Carty publicly apologized for "our failings" but the company said its mistakes never put passengers in danger. Investigators disagreed, citing problems dating back as far as 1995, including a

100-pound barrel of Dioxital left at the airport for three years.

Wednesday, September 8, 1999

ALL IN ALL, I'm frustrated. When I'm frustrated, I write. So I write to Denise Hedges, president of my union, the Association of Professional Flight Attendants. My letter complains of the lack of return phone calls from Emily Carter, the head of the APFA health department, and the attorney who would have represented me in my grievance.

In two months, my union has provided me with no legal assistance. Emily once called Juan to tell Juan she was on jury duty and couldn't return my phone call. But she never once called me. The attorney never called. As capable as Laura has been, she is not an attorney and doesn't have the legal education or experience.

I point out to Denise my concerns about the recent drug bust in Miami.

"After two months researching cocaine and drug testing, I know how dangerous the drug residue is to

241

people exposed unknowingly to it. I think I would call what was happening to our workforce reckless endangerment. At no time in the past two months was the cocaine smuggling ever brought to my attention while I discussed my case with various company departments and at no time has our work force been enlightened about the hazards in our working environment, in food carts, storage compartments, lavatories and galleys. I believe the questions raised by my test do have a broad impact on our workforce."

I outline how I've been to two substance abuse evaluations, had my own independent hair follicle test done and now been put on a drug monitoring program. I conclude: "I need the legal resources and support of our national staff."

A curt reply came Sept. 14 reply from Judith Ladislaw, vice president of our union. Her letter states that Laura Glading has kept her office informed of my termination proceedings.

"Not only has Ms. Glading provided you representation regarding your positive drug test, but she has spent numerous hours investigating each of your assertions surrounding the positive test result and then has, in very lengthy phone conversations, explained the outcome of her investigation to not only you but your roommate.

"Since random drug testing is a federally mandated policy, the criteria set out for programs following a positive test, whether the result was due to unknowing ingestion or not, is the same. I recommend that you follow the advice given by Ms. Glading regarding your employment."

Judy writes a column in the monthly APFA *Skyword* magazine about real flight attendant termination and on-the-job disciplinary cases, with names changed, and the ultimate outcome of their proceedings. She calls the column, "You Be the Judge." I feel crushed by the lack of compassion by our own Judge Judy and the lack of empathy by the leaders we elect to represent us.

For the $35 a month I pay in union dues, I feel I deserve better. My union in its constitution says it aims "to protect the individual and collective rights" of its members and that all members "shall have the right to due process and equal representation."

By e-mail I write back to Judy that she missed my point: that the case has broad impact and that I feel my union hasn't provided me with adequate resources. I have followed Laura's advice implicitly, right down to signing the reinstatement to get my job back. I also told her Roger is more than a "roommate," that he is a union rep and my life partner. I never get a follow-up response from Judge Judy. But then, I'm no longer surprised by anything. Months later, Judy is running in the APFA national election for president. She loses the election in a landslide vote.

In fact, at Laura's recommendation, I've written to Robert C. Ashby at the U.S. Department of Transportation in Washington. Laura wrote his name and address on a sheet of yellow legal paper the day I was terminated and suggested it might be the best way for me to fight my case.

Even if APFA can't support you, she told me, she would personally do everything she possibly could to assist me.

Weeks go by and I don't hear from Mr. Ashby or from APFA headquarters. The only new correspondence is a copy of the alleged second seal I receive from Laura. It's a mirror image of the initials and very blurry.

The silence is deafening. As far as both the company and union are concerned, I'm back at work. The case is closed. This is justice! For me, it will never be over until my name is cleared.

Friday, September 24, 1999

I'VE ALSO written to Elyse at EAP, sending her my work schedule from August so she can "monitor" my follow-up drug testing and as well as a letter informing her I will be moving to Lebanon, TN, in October and will need to have a testing site there.

The follow-up testing is one piece of baggage I have to take with me. It's a daily reminder. Every day I'm not at work, I pull the "Green Card" out of my wallet and dial up the drug testing system. When I haven't heard from Elyse in several weeks, I place a follow-up call. She tells me I will need to find my own drug testing site before I move since it was my choice to relocate.

"I don't even know where Lebanon is," she says. "And Tennessee is not part of my region."

She can't–or won't–offer any suggestion. It was my choice to relocate. Again, she says, she'll set up the billing with American Airlines once I find a lab to collect the samples.

"How am I supposed to do that?" I ask in a panic, amidst the boxes and packing we've started in anticipation of our move. "Doesn't American have some contract service for testing flight crews in Nashville?"

"Call around," she suggests curtly. "Check the Yellow Pages."

I check the hospital and medical listings in the relocation information sent by our real estate agent. The University Medical Center sounds like as good a possibility as any. When I reach the lab manager, I tell her what I need. She says I can be tested there 24 hours a day, seven days a week. I call Elyse back with her name and phone number.

Moving 1,200 miles two states away is complicated enough and this has been one added stress. We are strapped financially so there will be no professional movers for us. We're packing and moving ourselves.

The furniture will be loaded on Dickie's horse trailer and parked at his farm by the time our Virginia house is vacated. We'll haul the horses to Tennessee in our trailer and Dickie will follow with the furniture. For the 10 days in between homes, we'll stay in the living quarters of our horse trailer.

23

"Mistakes are part of the dues one pays for a full life."

–Sophia Loren

New York City
Tuesday, October 26, 1999

I'VE BEEN BACK at work two months, having transferred to New York's LaGuardia crew base and commuting from Nashville for every trip. Just when I think my life has settled down into a more normal routine, fallout from my nightmare surrounds me again.

I'm an unknown face here in New York. The anonymity at this crew base suits me. It's refreshing to not have so many coworkers inquiring about my troubles. After five months of upheaval, my financial state is just getting back to a resemblance of normalcy. The paychecks are regular and I have begun to pay off some debts from last summer.

I arrive one morning in New York several hours before my check-in and stop at my mailbox. I open an envelope from the payroll department, not knowing what it could be since payday is four days away. I'm shocked. It's a statement informing me that I owe the company $1,000-plus for sick time paid in error last summer.

I march into the office of the payroll administrator. She didn't know what the statement was when it arrived earlier in the morning. So I tell her my story and ask her to check when the payment will be deducted. She swivels around to her computer and pulls up my payroll record.

"This week?" I ask. "Without any advance notice? I won't have enough to cover my mortgage payment this week with all that taken out. They can't do this to me."

She says it's almost impossible to get payroll to reverse a payroll deduction this few days in advance because of a new computer system.

"If I have to pay back the company's error," I tell her, "the company can at least have the decency to work out a payment plan and give me a reasonable notice."

She says she'll call and try to get something worked out but can't promise anything. Later, she leaves a note in my mailbox telling me the deduction will be split between three paychecks, beginning this week.

THE PAYROLL problem is the result of a meeting I had a week ago with Duby Torres, my "attendance manager" in New York. I'm not happy so I go to her. She had called me in for an "attendance counseling" session. I called in sick in October, bringing my sick calls to twice in the past rolling 12 months. Company policy requires a meeting to make sure I understand the attendance policy. With five sick calls in nine years, do I look like I abuse the privilege of sick time?

At the time, I told Duby my whole story, that I really hadn't been sick in June, that the company removed me sick. All of flight service in Washington knew why I had been removed because I had told everyone who didn't know. My drug test is not a secret to me.

The attendance manager knew I was removed sick and I had told her why I had been removed when she was working on getting me back into the computer system. From the beginning, I suspected the sick removal had been in error. In fact, one union representative had told me *not* to mention it to anyone or I would be forced to pay it back.

Duby told me that if I wanted it removed, I should contact Elyse at EAP to have it switched to an EAP removal. I told her I was concerned that if I asked to have it corrected, I would probably be made to correct the pay error.

She said she wouldn't expect the company make me pay for someone else's mistake but that she would leave it up to me if I want to change the sick call or not.

I haven't called Elyse yet. I'm dumbfounded as to why the June error was suddenly fixed this week. I am more than angry. I am livid. I toss the payroll statement on her desk.

"Can you explain this?" I ask. "I haven't called Elyse and now the sick call has been removed from my attendance record. I thought you were going to leave it up to me?"

Duby seems as surprised as me. She copies the payroll statement and disappears down the hall. She's gone to confer with her boss. When she returns, she tells me last week she asked her boss, the base manager in New York, about my pay situation. The base manager contacted the base manager in Washington (Joy Simmons) who contacted crew scheduling who contacted someone in the payroll department who fixed the company error and never bothered to give me a decent notice.

Yikes! This information sure traveled faster than the paperwork to get me back on the payroll. In comparison, it's taken me two months to get my automatic bank deposit reactivated.

Not only do I have to pay back the company error, it cost me the opportunity to apply four weeks earlier for unemployment benefits. Since I was still being "paid" sick, I was not eligible to seek unemployment.

And unemployment benefits cannot be sought retroactively. Now I have neither sick pay nor unemployment for those weeks.

"I'm terribly sorry this happened," Duby says. "I never expected that to happen. In five years, I've never seen something like this happen before."

"Welcome to my nightmare," I tell her. "In other words, if I meet with you about an attendance concern, it's not confidential. It's between you, me and everyone else in the company."

"It's probably no consolation to you," adds Duby, "but Joy (Simmons) is retiring at the end of the year."

A WEEK LATER, a flight services secretary for American Eagle pilots in Dallas calls me at home. A pilot in Texas has been receiving my company mail at his home. She traced my phone number from crew scheduling.

We can't figure out why my mail is going to his home. His address is not similar, nor are our employee numbers. I place calls to make sure the various benefits and payroll departments have my correct address. Chalk up one more corporate fiasco.

24

"And so it goes."
–Linda Ellerbee

Lebanon, Tenn.
Tuesday, November 23, 1999

THE PHONE rings. It's for Roger. It's one of his union reps. A flight attendant at USAirways has been suspended from service after a random drug test. Roger was called because of his knowledge about drug testing learned in my case. The lab reported that this flight attendant's specimen couldn't be tested, that it was "non human," whatever that means.

This is a new scenario to both of us. Either there is a testing error or the sample was switched. The credibility of the flight attendant and the circumstances of the test suggests that the sample was proper though she drank a lot of water before providing it.

In either case, there is more research to do. Roger is on the phone again. Turns out she was not the first flight attendant who has had this experience. Two Delta flight attendants were fired under similar circumstances this year.

IN SEPTEMBER 1998, the Department of Transportation (DOT) issued new guidelines to laboratories and Medical Review Officers responsible for conducting drug testing programs. The new procedures gave reporting standards found "adulterated," "diluted" or "substitute." The DOT hopes to identify people thwarting drug testing by adding water or other substances to their sample. The guidelines are not mandatory but establish thresholds and reporting standards. Indeed, entire Internet sites are devoted to cheating the drug testing system by blocking drug analyses. Products are sold for this express purpose.

Under the DOT directive, urine samples first undergo a screen for specific gravity and creatine content. The method assumes a sample "consistent with normal human urine" will exhibit a specific gravity equal or greater than 1.001 and contain creatine content of greater or equal to 5 mg/dl. Creatine is a metabolite produced in correlation with your total body muscle mass. It gathers in your blood stream until cleared from your system by the kidneys.

In theory, a sample legitimately originating from the body would possess at least the threshold creatine quantity in a spot sample (one time voiding) of urine. Creatine production is a medical test your doctor might order to analyze your kidney health. However, it's interesting to note that a doctor doesn't normally order a spot sample. Such a sample has too much variation and is considered relatively worthless. Rather, the standard test for kidney function is to collect a 24-hour production of urine.

Under DOT guidelines, a sample containing creatine less than or equal to 5 mg/dl and a specific gravity of less than or equal to 1.001 is ruled "substitute" and no further testing is conducted. A "substitute" sample is never tested for the presence of illegal drugs. The procedures do not incorporate safeguards. A sample judged substitute is considered a "refusal to test." Case closed. No follow up medical evaluation of the individual is performed. No questions are asked. No appeal is allowed.

The flight attendants who have had a sample judged "substitute" all have more in common than their airline jobs. They are all female, take vitamin supplements, are vegetarian or seldom eat meat products. If you drink large amounts of water and are small without a lot of muscle mass, you are a prime candidate to have the same thing happen to you.

The USAirways flight attendant, after being suspended, evaluated for substance abuse and re-tested, was returned to work in two weeks with back pay. That action was prompted by the timely pressure, support and resources provided by her union, the Association of Flight Attendants (AFA), led in a team effort by Mollie McCarthy in Baltimore.

The company admitted because of the flight attendant's high level of cooperation and her dedication to completing the evaluation so quickly, "we have elected to make an exception in your case and pay you for all time lost." The company called her case "unique. Although your random test was considered a refusal under Federal regulations, the company was unable to determine conclusively whether you had adultered or otherwise tampered with the specimen you provided."

In dramatic contrast, the Delta flight attendants, who do not have union representation, are still fighting their cases. (Interestingly, federal regulations do not require termination under this rule.) One of the Delta flight attendants, who is Japanese, says, "I have no fancy explanation or reason because I am innocent. I can't think of any reason that I would jeopardize my career here by something like this."

Delta officials acknowledged that the samples were never tested for drugs but maintain that a "tough line" is necessary to ensure a safe airline.

Delta pilots, campaigning on behalf of the flight attendants, aren't questioning the accuracy of the test but rather if the science is sound, a question not answered by the FAA. They ask: Is 5 mg/dl of creatine a threshold that no innocent person could go below?

A study conducted by the Addiction Research Center in Baltimore in 1994 confirms the science. When study participants drank one gallon of water, specific gravity fell to very low levels (less than 1.003) and creatine fell to less than 20 mg/dl in one hour. Just drinking 12 ounces of water was enough to cause a significant drop in both.

(Two years later in the Delta case, a jury awarded flight attendant Yasuko Ishikawa $400,000 after the lab that conducted the drug test was found negligent. She was reinstated.)

25

"All of our dreams can come true if we have the courage to pursue them."

–Walt Disney

Thanksgiving Day, 1999

MANY QUESTIONS remain unanswered about last summer. Perhaps I'll never have all the answers. Am I angry? Yes. Am I bitter? Yes. But I have found peace. I *know* the truth. Just because company authorities or my union leaders weren't convinced by the evidence–medical as well as circumstantial–doesn't validate their position anymore than mine.

My hair follicle test came up negative to a lower test standard (5 ng) than the urinalysis yields. My random test showed a low level (219 and 202 ng) compared to both the FAA standard (150 ng) and other positive tests ran in the lab on the same day as mine. The preliminary screening cutoff is even higher at 300 ng. How did my low level specimen get past the screening?

Was I exposed to a low level of cocaine on money I took for a cocktail on the airplane? Was I exposed to drug residue spilled in a food cart or in a galley onto something I ate or drank that day? Was it the procaine I used in treating sick horses? Did anyone in a position of medical authority ever thoroughly examine my evidence? No. Is there any indication that I have ever used cocaine or any other illicit drug in my life? No. You can draw your own conclusion.

Is the science foolproof? We would like to believe the medical world is infallible. We know it's not.

Medical errors kill more Americans than traffic accidents, breast cancer or AIDS, according to the Institute of Medicine, an independent body that makes recommendations to Congress.

A study out in November estimates from 44,000 to 98,000 deaths a year attributed to medical mistakes, making it the eighth leading cause of death. Many of the errors are attributed to "systems failures." Some are as simple as giving the wrong drug to the incorrect diagnoses. Medical science is only as good as the humans behind it.

More than ever, I'm convinced there are major weaknesses in workplace drug testing. A *USA Today* editorial argues that current drug testing techniques are outdated. The editorial cites incidents that threatened public safety because the current urinalysis used failed to catch savvy drug offenders. A drug user knows the foreign substances that disrupt the test or destroy the presence of a drug.

USA Today suggests that the DOT has been dragging its feet on the more reliable hair testing for drugs, a technology that been around for a decade and provides a view of drug use up to three months.

Hair testing is used by the Federal Reserve, more than a thousand private businesses and increasing number of police agencies. New York City's police department detected five times the number of drug users among its recruits with hair tests than it did with urine tests, and at 30 times the rate among probationary officers. Boston's police department reported finding 23 drug users on its force that urinalysis had missed.

I'M MOVING ON, but I'm not forgetting. I sit in my new office looking out the front window at our three horses grazing peacefully in their field among the Cedar and oak trees. Pregnant Honey, as wide as her stall door, is due with her foal in four months. Life is good. I'm moving on.

Roger is preparing Thanksgiving dinner for guests arriving in a few hours. They've been stranded most of the day at the Charlotte airport. Our two new dogs (Roger asked God to send us "farm" dogs and we already have two delivered by a neighbor) are chasing each other around the yard.

I unpacked some Christmas decorations this morning and strung multicolored lights on the front of our log home as we begin the first holiday season in our new home. I smell a fire burning in the fireplace and a turkey and fixin's cooking in the kitchen.

There's more work to do here in the country than we ever thought possible. A half-dozen moving boxes haven't been opened and unpacked yet. There are trees and underbrush to cut, grass to be mowed, fences to repair and build, a riding ring to put up and the barn to be repaired. We need new carpeting and a new refrigerator. Rooms and closets to be remodeled and updated. These are challenges for my hands and back. I enjoy the physical labor. I've always found satisfaction in creating, building and fixing things. Is this my new reality?

I am an early riser now. No more lounging in bed until 10 am. I wake up to the sounds of birds, maybe a neighbor's dog barking in the distance or a cow bellowing for its calf. No more annoying car alarms in the neighborhood, no more traffic, no more horns blaring, no more police and fire sirens.

Outside my window as we enjoy our morning coffee are blue jays, woodpeckers, chickadees and at least six cardinals. (I thought the cardinal was the *Virginia* state bird?) One of the new neighbors gave us a bird feeder for a housewarming present.

We packed the worry dolls in Virginia and haven't taken them out again. The "Serenity Prayer"

Christmas decoration we set out in the living room every year says it all: "God, Grant me the Serenity to accept the things I cannot change, the Courage to change the things I can, and Wisdom to know the difference."

As a compassionate colleague on an airplane this fall told me, "Tragedy doesn't change who you are, it shows who you are."

26

"We know information has healing power. The best way to heal a wrong is to shine a light on it."

–Philip Meyer, Knight Chair, University of North Carolina, in *USA Today*

AFTER writing four times to the Department of Transportation (DOT) and not receiving any response, I enlisted the assistance of my U.S. Senators from Tennessee. Their inquiries to the DOT prompted a response to me from Robert C. Ashby that arrived in late March 2000, seven months after my first letter:

"I apologize for the delay in responding...You asked whether there is an appeal or complaint process at the Department of Transportation in cases of positive drug tests.

"As your correspondence notes, there are a number of safeguards available to employees who test positive for drugs. Under the Department of Transportation's testing procedures, you asked for,

and received, a test of a split specimen at a second laboratory. Under your union's agreement with American Airlines, you had access to a grievance proceeding concerning the test. The Department of Transportation, however, does not have an administrative appeal or complaint mechanism that could review or overturn the result of a drug test conducted by a transportation employer under the Department's rules…"

I am dumbfounded. The appeal process recommended by my union is nonexistent. I signed the reinstatement on the basis of planning a direct appeal to the DOT. That the test results stand without an appeal through the DOT and that I returned to work doesn't mean the test is correct.

In the past year, I've been drug tested 20 times on my days off, all with a negative result. This has to end. My daily routine is regularly interrupted by the requirement to drive 20 miles into the hospital to be tested.

A few weeks after hearing from Mr. Ashby, we took my case to Stedman's, a drug and alcohol testing company that provides services in custody cases, churches, schools, businesses and law enforcement agencies. The firm in Bensalem, Penn., was recommended to us by the Association of Flight Attendants (AFA), Roger's union, not mine.

Roger reaches Dr. Wasim Anwar, who represents Stedman's and legal firms on issues arising out of positive drug test results. He is a medical doctor, health care educator and drug addiction counselor. He agrees to review the litigation packages and chain of custody documents in my case.

Several weeks later, he has found problems in my case, several minor and one major problem. Minor concerns include initials of a certifying official that should have been a signature, a missing name and address of the certifying official and log numbers that have been changed. Also, two different certifying scientists are listed. One report lists Mary Hightower; another shows Hai Nguyen as the certifying scientist.

But most ominous is the concentration levels of the split sample. The computer-generated lab reports a level of 101.575 but certifying scientist Mary

Hightower, in handwriting, has multiplied this number by two to get a quantitative result of 202.

As Dr. Anwar points out, a level of 101 does not meet the DOT cutoff for a positive test and would be thrown out. He sees no apparent justification for the multiplying factor. "What positive test?" he asks Roger rhetorically.

To us, it appears the data was manipulated to assure that the split test confirmed the first test. Interestingly, Cindy Buff at AA Medical warned us that a split has never come up different than the original.

A FEW DAYS LATER, we're on our way to meet Timothy Davis, a local attorney who has agreed to take my case. I feel encouraged by our first meeting. We've actually found someone who believes an injustice has occurred and he's willing to take on the fight. Roger and I spend several hours discussing the case and he picks several focus points.

Tim Davis drafts a brief letter to Dr. David McKenas, American Airlines medical director, on May

10, 2000. He points out several problems with the chain of custody of the split test.

"I have informed my client of the possible legal remedies he possesses in this situation, I also told him I felt communicating with you first could possibly get the result he desires without litigating the issue," Tim writes. "My client's sole purpose is to clear his name. We're hoping you can help us move forward to accomplish that."

A month later, Tim hears from Francis Heil, an attorney for American Airlines, who refutes the few issues we outlined to him. He writes that he does not agree with the concerns over the drug test and notes that my union, a collective bargaining group, has specific provisions for challenging the drug test case.

After we meet with Tim again, he drafts a letter directly to Francis Heil. This letter questions different points, the signatures versus initials, differing certifying scientists, and the time stamps on the chain of custody documents at the two labs.

Tim writes that his client "is not simply someone who got caught with his hand in the cookie jar, rather a devoted employee of 10 years with American Airlines. Mr. Ritter is a person of strong morals and outstanding character. This is why we are questioning what we feel are the discrepancies within the chain of custody and the testing itself."

Tim concludes: "My client still is subjected to random tests, sometimes as many as three a week. My client is the one who knows, within in his heart of hearts, he did not do anything wrong. As an attorney, I sometimes get jaded to the 'I'm innocent' pleas of clients. I do not feel Mr. Ritter is posturing or misleading us. I feel he is an honest person who wants his life back. At this point he can't be made whole again, but he can be made right."

The wait begins. Months pass. We check in with Tim periodically. When Tim's follow-up calls to Francis Heil are returned, Tim is assured that a response is forthcoming. Six months will pass and there will be no follow-up letter from American Airlines.

Ironically, the only letter I receive from my company is a congratulatory letter upon my "milestone" completion of 10 years of service in June. "You may look back on your years of service and know you contributed directly to your Company's leadership," states the letter from Flight Service management. "Congratulations on your anniversary and thanks for the important part you have played in the corporation's success."

Saturday, Dec. 16, 2000

THE Department of Transportation announces new rules for drug testing procedures. The new rules address concerns over creatine levels, allowing a physician hired by the employer to cancel finding of tampering if that result comes from a legitimate medical reason. In other words, a low creatine level will no longer be an automatic indicator that the donor tampered with the specimen.

The same day, the Department of Health and Human Services disclosed new evidence of lab mistakes that can brand innocent workers as cheaters or drug abusers, ending their careers without a chance for appeal.

HHS reported that it inspected all 66 of the validity testing laboratories it supervises. As a result, the HHS instructed labs to cancel the results of tests failed by 250 to 300 workers, according to news reports.

While my case does not involve creatine levels, I find this announcement encouraging. It acknowledges that existing drug testing rules are not foolproof and that appropriate changes can be made in the way DOT conducts workplace drug testing.

January 2001

HARD AS it is to believe, it's been 19 long months since that day in Miami when I was pulled off my trip and sent home to Washington, DC. Now our life centers around our country home and our animals. We made improvements on the house and started building new wood fences. Dickie and Denise have purchased a property just five miles away and will be our Tennessee "neighbors" in a few months.

Roger and I have both transferred to the international flying operations of our respective companies. The first time I flew to Paris, Roger met me there and we enjoyed cafe au lait on a street corner, took pictures of the Eiffel Tower and enjoyed a great French dinner.

One morning at home Roger and I are discussing my drug testing case, as we frequently do over our morning coffee. *What have we missed? Who are the players that could properly address our questions? Where do we go next with my case?*

Roger recalls a telephone conversation from more than a year ago with Patrice Kelly in the Drug Abatement Division of the Federal Aviation Administration (FAA). He decides to touch base with her again. She remembers the earlier phone conversation and seems interested in the information we've collected. She tells Roger that the FAA Drug Abatement Division can investigate a drug testing case and refers us to Karen Leamon, manager of the program policy branch.

In a January 25, 2001 letter, I outline my case and request an investigation. Among the irregularities I point out: initials versus the required signature of certifying scientists, two different certifying scientists on different documents, the split test of 101 that was manipulated by hand to get a 202 result and the wide difference in how many times the two different labs handled my tests.

"I cannot over stress how much in error this test was since I have never and would never use illicit drugs of any kind," I write. "I am concerned about the scientific basis of test levels, accountability of individuals from the labs to the medical review officers. No innocent person should suffer like this because a government program or rule is so inadequate and so obviously fails to recognize the truth."

Weeks go by and we anxiously watch the mail for an answer. When I haven't received a response after several months, Roger writes a follow-up letter to Patrice Kelly. A March 27 letter from the FAA acknowledges my request: "The investigation is still open, so we are unable to provide you with any information at this time until the investigation is completed."

By June I haven't heard back from the FAA. I write to U.S. Senators Bill Frist and Fred Thompson from Tennessee, seeking help a second time to get a federal agency to respond to my questions. Subsequent correspondence from them gives me hope that the investigation will be completed by the end of the summer.

July 2001

Meanwhile, we continue to meet with our attorney to discuss legal remedies. On July 17, we file suit in Wilson County Circuit Court, naming Dr. David McKenas, medical director of American Airlines, the defendant. The claim: McKenas was negligent in failing to provide due care in overseeing the testing process or to investigate new evidence provided to him.

The suit asks for $2.2 million for damages for pain and suffering in the past and in the future, depression, nervousness, financial strain, loss of appetite, loss of self-esteem and loss of sleep in the past and "loss of capacity of the enjoyment of life in the past, and loss of enjoyment of life in the future…"

By midAugust, the suit is kicked to U.S. District Court in Nashville and a seven-page response from the defendant's attorneys asks for dismissal based on personal jurisdiction, lack of proper venue, and applicable statute of limitation, among a total of 22 defenses. None of the defenses address the science of drug testing, the real heart of my concerns.

While we wait for the lawsuit to play out, the FAA concludes its investigation. The letter arrives in the mail in late August.

In response to my concerns about hair follicle testing, the FAA states that the MRO cannot consider tests conducted outside the scope of DOT regulations since the DOT and FAA only recognize drug-testing procedures approved by the Department of Health and Human Services (i.e. urinalysis).

"Because your other concerns are with the laboratories that processed your specimen and American Airlines' polices, your appeal would be with American Airlines," states Diane Wood, Manager, Drug Abatement Division, FAA. "FAA inspectors do not evaluate laboratory procedures. This responsibility lies with HHS."

The end of August also marks the two-year anniversary of my "continuous drug-monitoring program," the daily telephone checks on my drug testing. The frequency of the required tests seems to have waned in recent months. I was tested once in June, not at all in July and, most recently, August 1. I haven't heard from the EAP office as how the end will happen. When I reach Laverne Washington, Elyse's replacement, he says he'll have to check "the book" as to when I started to determine if I've completed the required 48 months.

"I signed my reinstatement August 13, and returned to work on August 22," I tell Laverne.

"You know the dates?" he asks.

"Of course. I had already had my first follow-up test by the end of August 1999."

"If that's the case, you're done at the end of this month," he says.

"You mean I can just stop calling?" I ask.

"Yep." We chat cordially about the long two years I've been through and say good-by for the last time.

No hoopla. No celebration. Not even a congratulatory letter that all my tests in the past two years came up "clean." The closure has emptiness to it. *At least that chapter of the nightmare is over.*

At the same time, our attorney, Tim Davis, has met in Nashville with attorneys for the defendant. The discussions focus on the legal maneuvers, not drug testing. We meet with Tim to discuss our options and respond to the defenses. We have reasonable responses to nearly all the defenses, but some areas of our legal position are gray. Nonetheless, Tim's mood is grim. He advises us to consider withdrawing the suit at this time until a new approach can be found.

Buenos Aires, Argentina
Tuesday, Sept. 11, 2001

THE PHONE in my hotel room rings. "Are you awake, John?" the purser from my crew asks. "Do you have your television on?"

I don't. The news is confusing, she says. Two airline jets have crashed into the twin towers of the World Trade Center in New York. America is under attack.

I turn my television to CNN and pull on jeans and a T-shirt without showering. I head to the lobby crew lounge and join other crewmembers in front of the television. A third jet has crashed into the Pentagon and a fourth is "missing" in Pennsylvania. Two of the planes belong to American Airlines. No word on the other two. Thus, we join the country in vigil as we watch the terrorist tragedy unfold on television. We knew it would be days before we would return to the United States. Our jobs and our lives are changed forever.

I know my family is worried about me and I am worried about Roger. He was scheduled to be working a flight from London to Philadelphia this morning. Not sure who I should call, so I place a phone call to Tennessee where I reach a machine at Dickie and Denise's house.

I leave a message for Denise, asking her to call my mother and let her know my whereabouts, keep an eye on our dogs and horses and let Roger know I am okay if she hears from him. The next day I finally hear from Roger, whose flight had left London, then returned to London after the incidents in America.

As days go by, I discover a "cyber café" near the hotel and communicate via e-mail with Denise and others back in the U.S. We try to take our minds off the tragedy by shopping and lunching, but it's nearly impossible to think or talk about anything else.

Seven days later, Roger and I both arrive home from our trips. We've given Tim Davis the go-ahead to withdraw our suit "without prejudice," giving us a year to take it up again if we can figure out a better legal position. Now is not a good time to be going after an airline in court. My drug testing tragedy seems miniscule compared to the world tragedy we just suffered through.

A few weeks later, I get a note from Tim, who expresses his shared disappointment that we could not proceed on the case, and his bill. "I also understand having to pay the remaining legal fees will be an even more bitter end to this saga," he acknowledges. "I am willing to work with you on these charges…"

The phone rings. It's for Roger. A union rep with the Association of Flight Attendants. I listen as he asks questions. The sound of grave concern in his voice rings familiar to my ears. I can tell from hearing just half the conversation that a flight attendant at USAirways has tested positive for cocaine in a random drug test.

From what Roger is saying, the case must be similar to mine. Proclaimed guilty, but with reason to believe there is an error. I fear the future this flight attendant faces. The monster drug test rears its ugly head again.

John Ritter

Epilogue

THE IMPULSE to write *A Trace Element* began with the simple chronology I wrote for my termination conference. In writing a journal of what was happening to me, I attempted to sort out the facts. My life was chaos. A few sheets of paper quickly turned into a box full of file folders. However, every question led to more questions.

My hope is that by raising questions, this book will raise consciousness about illegal drugs and drug testing. Those of us who don't live in a drug-using environment are fairly naïve and have mostly superficial knowledge about drugs.

My dream is that this book will educate workers who are subject to drug testing about the pitfalls, the real danger of second-hand or involuntary exposure and the importance of being acutely aware of your environment and proper procedures when you are selected for a drug test. Not using illegal drugs is simply not enough.

I was hurt by a drug test that went wrong. I lost my job. But I was more fortunate than many. I returned to work early in this two-year odyssey and I pursued my dreams. I feel better to have told my story – the humbling and embarrassing moments along with the exhilarating incidents.

It's been a healing and "coming out" experience in itself to be public about a private matter such as workplace drug testing. Being in the midst of supportive people saved me. I had assurance that I was supported and believed. I want others to know they're not alone.

I see this book not as the end, but a beginning, the groundwork to a foundation or organization that can help individuals who have drug addiction problems and innocent victims caught in the web of drug testing.

Appendix

What Drugs Will Cause a Positive Drug Test Result?

MOST PRESCRIPTION medicine will not cause a positive drug test. For example, AZT, lithium, antidepressants, antibiotics, tranquilizers, sleeping pills, medicine with caffeine, and medications for diabetes and epilepsy will not show up in a workplace drug screen. Legitimate explanations for positive test results on initial screening, according to the National Institute on Drug Abuse, include the following:

Marijuana: THC can be used as an anti medic for cancer chemotherapy patients with intractable vomiting. Passive inhalation of marijuana will not explain a positive test because the cutoff for the first test is 100 ng/ML. Only prescription use is acceptable.

Cocaine: It is useful as an anesthetic and vasoconstrictor for certain types of surgery involving the nose, throat, larynx and lower respiratory passages. Only dosages administered by doctors or dentists are acceptable. Some herbal teas could cause a false positive, though the FDA has ordered them off the market.

Amphetamines: Although they can be used to treat narcolepsy, attention-deficit disorder, depression that has not responded to other treatments, and obesity, their use is controversial because of the risk of abuse.

Amphetamine-related drugs, e.g. asthma medication with ephedrine (Azpan, Bronkaid, Bronkolixir, Bronkotabs, Mudrane, Pazo, Primatine P&M, Auadrinal, Tedral, Theozine, Vatronol, Wyanoids), over-the-counter cold and hay fever medication with phenylpropanolamine (A.R.M., Acutrim, Alka-Seltzer Plus, Allerest, Appedrine, Bayer Children's Cold Tabs and Cough Syrup, CCP Tablets, Cheracol Plus, Chexit, Children's CoTylenol, Comtrex, Contac, Control, Dexatrim, Dietac, Demetapp, Dristan, Robitussin, Ru-Tuss, Sinarest, Sine-off, Sinubid, S-T Forte, St. Joseph's Cold Tablets for Children, Sucrets, Super Odrinex, Triaminin, Triaminicin, Triaminicol, Trind, Tussagesic) and some vasodilators may produce a false positive test. These lists should not be considered complete.

However, the Medical Review Officer (MRO) is advised to carefully question individuals testing positive for amphetamines about their over-the-counter and prescribed medications.

Opiates: Many prescription drugs contain codeine or morphine and will produce a "true" positive opiate result. These include Ambenyl Cough Syrup, Bromphen-DC Expectorant, Dimetane, Dolprn #3, Naldecon, Nvahistine, Robitussin A-C, Triafed-C, Roxanol, Percocet, Percodar and Tylox, as well as any medication containing codeine. A legitimate prescription, which explains the test result, means the MRO must report the test as negative. Some cough suppressing and antidiarrheal preparations contain paregoric with sufficient anhydrous morphine to produce a morphine or morphine/codeine positive test.

Recent ingestion of poppy seeds, such as in a bagel or muffin, also may cause a positive urine test for opiates. Before the MRO can verify a confirmed positive test for opiates (which does not indicate heroin use), the MRO must find other signs of drug abuse. The MRO likely will direct the employee to the medical department to submit to examination for needle tracks or signs of intoxication or withdrawal, or report the test as negative.

Phencyclidine (PCP): It has no therapeutic role and therefore no legitimate excuse for positive test results.

THE PENALTY for refusing to submit to a drug test, regardless of the reason, will be as severe as a positive test itself: suspension and probable termination. This might include failing to provide a urine specimen or a sufficient quantity for testing, refusing to report to a test site within the time period specified or substituting or adulterating a specimen.

It's not worth the cost, even if it means getting home later than expected after work. Or, if it requires hours and drinking plenty of water to provide the necessary urine specimen because you just recently urinated, that's what it requires.

At American Airlines, an employee who refuses to test or fails to follow a directive to test will be withheld from service without pay, pending investigation, according to policy. If the investigation confirms the refusal to follow a drug-testing directive, the employee will be terminated for violating the company rule under insubordination. The employee also would be referred to a Substance Abuse Professional.

John Ritter